THE IMPACT OF ONE VOICE, VOLUME II

INSPIRATIONAL STORIES OF PASSION, PURPOSE, AND PERSEVERANCE

Published by
Hybrid Global Publishing
333 E 14th Street
#3C
New York, NY 10003

Manufactured in the United States of America, or in the United Kingdom when distributed elsewhere.

Robinson, Arvee.
The Impact of One Voice, Volume II
ISBN: 978-1-957013-99-2
eBook: 978-1-961757-00-4

Cover design by: Natasha Clawson
Copyediting by: Claudia Volkman
Interior design by: Suba Murugan

ArveeRobinson.com

CONTENTS

INTRODUCTION

Arvee Robinson

Our voice is our biggest asset, yet often we are silenced. Whether it is because of culture, childhood, or gender, it happens to all of us at some point in our lives. During this silence, we experience the loss of our voice and often feel powerless.

This book is a community of voices coming together to speak their truth and make an impact with their words. In some cases, these are the voices of the voiceless. These pages are full of stories demonstrating courage and triumph over what may seem impossible life situations.

As authors, speakers, and storytellers, we pray that our words will make an impact on our readers and listeners. Whether we know it or not, they will make an impact on someone at some point. On rare occasions, we may even get the privilege of finding out just how much.

This is one of those rare occasions.

Inside these pages, you will find inspirational stories that will feed your soul, challenge your mind, and leave you with the feeling of blissfulness.

You, too, have a voice.

Trust that *your* story about passion, purpose, and perseverance will change lives and create *infinite impact*.

LIVE IN THE LIGHT

Tiffany S. Beall

"Well done, good and faithful servant; you were faithful over a few things, I will make you ruler over many things. Enter into the joy of your Lord."

—Matthew 25:21

A leader, teacher, friend, minister, missionary, prayer partner, and dedicated Christian are some of the characteristics that describe my father, Bishop Rev. Dr. Charles Eugene Henderson. I first met the man who would later become my father when I was a little girl, at the age of five years old. He attended a cookout held for my mother at her cousin's house in Texas. Both my soon-to-be stepdad and my mom were grieving the recent loss of their deceased spouses. My mom and I met a friendly, kind Christian man who helped me retrieve the basketball that accidentally rolled out of my hands into the pool. My mother and my stepdad got to know each other through a long-distance telephone relationship over the course of the next few months. Later that year, they married in California.

My dad was a Christian minister who believed in God and had strong faith. He taught me and others through his approximately fifty years of missionary work what it means to be a strong Christian. He taught the value of living a separated, dedicated, and consecrated life as a follower of Jesus Christ.

Charles was the eldest son in his large family in Texas. He wanted to make sure his family members believed in Jesus Christ as their Lord and Savior. At a very young age, he would stand on a wash basin and imitate his pastor preaching a sermon. He wanted his family members to know what it meant to be a Christian, and he had an enthusiastic and captive audience. Preaching to his family members was the inception of his preaching, pastoring, and ministry days.

He was officially called to the ministry at the age of nineteen. My dad feared God and the potential punishment for living a life different from the godly teachings found in the Bible. Charles was mentored by renowned Christian teachers and ministers and attended Bible colleges, including Christ for the Nations and Evangel Christian University, to gain a better understanding of the Bible and to learn the deeper things of God. God used my dad's knowledge to teach people about the Word of God and reach people for Christ. He helped many people better understand that God wants to help them reach their fullest potential and work in the light of Christ. For many years, he taught people recovering from substance abuse how to live a clean life, free from alcohol and drug addiction.

Many opportunities came as he helped pastors and ministers expand their ministries. My dad taught the Bible to people on the ranch, at work, at church, and wherever he could. After hearing my dad on a Christian radio broadcast in Texas, one of his friends said that my dad said more in fifteen minutes about the Bible and the Lord than many people said in an hour.

My dad loved to teach. He often shared the "four-legged stool of doing things at the right time, in the right place, and in the right manner, which will give you the right results." He would ride along with law enforcement officers as a counselor and support, helping youth and adults who were involved in gangs to choose a better way to live. Another one of his sayings was "God has a wonderful plan and purpose for your life."

My dad was a diligent worker. When he was younger, my dad had no choice but to work hard and not take breaks; there was too much work to do on the farm. There was just as much work to do in the city when he was older and his family moved to the city.

He shined shoes, caddied for golfers, worked at the local theater, and performed many other jobs. During high school, he was all-around athlete, playing baseball and basketball, running track and field, swimming, and becoming a football star. He helped lead his team at A.J. Moore High School to win championships. He married after he graduated from high school and moved to Dallas, Texas, where he worked hard and focused on studying the Bible. He had a gifted memory and could quote and understand a plethora of Bible scriptures.

My dad learned what it meant to be humble like Moses and the Apostle Paul. Sometimes my dad's thorns in his flesh were people in the church. My dad was gifted in leadership and different ministerial roles, and people in authority at different churches tried to hinder him from following the call that God placed upon his life. As my dad listened to the leading of the Holy Spirit, he would sometimes lead people away from traditions found in the church. Rev. Henderson led church members according to God's word and changed situations for the better. He lived by completely placing his faith and trust in God for help and guidance. His dependence upon following the Lord's word sometimes meant that some people would permanently leave the church. The Bible says that "without faith, it is impossible to please God." My dad depended upon God to lead him as he helped establish churches and strengthen and grow churches in the United States and throughout the world. He helped Filipino, Nigerian, Ghanaian, African, Indian, American, and many other national and international Christian churches become more established in the word of God.

My father founded Love Ministries International World Outreach more than thirty years ago. My dad also worked very closely with the Association of Evangelical Gospel Assemblies (AEGA). Working in other countries with these two ministries afforded our family opportunities to be involved with orphanages and schools at all education levels, providing glasses and medical equipment and performing other missionary work.

Dr. Henderson was a gifted teacher and would usually travel to Africa at least once a year. The cry of my father's heart was to see that each country he visited had clean, safe drinking water. He was able to fundraise for years to have water wells dug in Nigeria and to have water piped in from natural springs in Kenya. He and my mom spearheaded many other fundraising opportunities to get American organizations and churches involved in gathering and sharing clean clothing, books, medical supplies and equipment, transportation vehicles, and musical instruments to Côte D'Ivoire (Ivory Coast, West Africa).

My dad was a trailblazer. He was the first African-American to hold roles in different Christian and business companies and organizations. He owned a roofing and remodeling business and a gas station that sold food items in Dallas. He brought his business skills to California and helped many people with varying needs. My dad accumulated treasures in heaven throughout his life and accomplished many things as a servant of Christ helping many people.

Bishop Charles Henderson had faith that if God permitted him, he would live to be 120 years old like Moses in the Bible. He prayed for other people who were ill or had physical deformities; my dad knew that God is able to heal any illness. The other main thorn in his flesh became his health challenges and physical ailments during the last few years of his life.

My dad wanted to help ministers throughout the world grow closer to the Lord, understand the Bible better, and help the members of their congregations become stronger Christians. He taught for more than fifty years, and recordings of his radio, television, and sermon teachings and messages are available to teach others who God is and how He wants us to live a good and holy life. Rev. Henderson was a good shepherd in the ministry who treated people with love and respect.

Dr. Charles Henderson loved people and was passionate about inspiring them to live a good life. He wanted everyone to know that they could learn more about the Lord, become Christians, and be free of contentious behavior and divisions. He always taught people that God is a God of order, and that we need to ask God to help us get our lives in order.

I am still a work in progress, but because of what I learned from my father's good life through his love for my mom, me, our family, our friends, and our fellow human beings, I have a great example of how to live my life as a Christian. I am sure my dad received the commendation from Jesus found in Matthew 25:34-36, "Then the King will say to those on His right hand, 'Come, you blessed of My Father, inherit the kingdom prepared for you from the foundation of the world: for I was hungry and you gave Me food; I was thirsty and you gave Me drink; I was a stranger and you took Me in; I was naked and you clothed Me; I was sick and you visited Me; I was in prison and you came to Me.'"

Be a light to and in your surroundings. Ask yourself, "What can I do and how can I make the lives of others around me better? How can I serve and love others more, regardless of their relationship with me? How can my life shine and be a light in this world, in my environment? What changes in my life do I need to make for my light to shine?"

Tiffany S. Beall has dedicated her life to serving people. She volunteers at hospitals and nursing homes, and she performs local and international missionary work in the United States and Africa. She volunteered as a missionary for many years with her parents' ministry, Love Ministry International World Outreach. She graduated from Northwestern University with a bachelor of science in biomedical engineering and a minor degree in business institutions. Tiffany later received a master of science and PhD in natural medicine from Kingdom College of Natural Health. She has used her knowledge of medicine and business wherever she worked to help others with various challenges. She also has a passion to help people understand the importance of being financially literate.

A few years ago, she started working with Chris L. Ward and his real estate investment business, Memshalah Enterprises, LLC. That same year she started a company called Biz Intersect, Inc. which is designed to connect different business and financial companies and ventures together. She also began learning about becoming a digital content publisher. Currently, she is working on publishing for different websites.

Tiffany enjoys reading, doing various forms of artwork, playing the piano, and singing. She continues to share truths and provide assistance through volunteer and Christian work. The nonprofit ministry founded by her parents is still an important part of her life. She desires to share the biblical truths taught by her father, Bishop Rev. Dr. Charles E. Henderson through Love Ministries.

www.LoveMinistriesIntl.com

LOVING AGAINST ALL ODDS

Lorena Coello

In many ways I have always been proud, audacious, and courageous. It is what catapulted me to starting a business at age twenty-two without having a clue. Looking back at my life, however, I faced some big obstacles. My biggest challenge was speaking up to people with narcissistic behavior. I was spinning my wheels, going nowhere fast in my efforts to understand this issue. I struggled to express my emotions in a respectful and amicable manner. I found that people with narcissistic behavior were good people but with strong, overpowering personalities that made them extremely intimidating.

The first time I spoke up to narcissistic behavior was with my mother. Before she kicked me out at age fifteen, for years I babysat my younger brothers. I didn't mind, since I loved them as my own children. As I got older, I moved back to the attic of my mother's house to save money and work on my business. One day, she asked me to babysit a handicapped boy she was supposed to watch. The excuse was that her friend was in desperate need of help and had an emergency. At first, I said yes. But when this friend arrived, I noticed her teased hair, heavy makeup, high heels, and tiny mini skirt. I told my mother I would not watch the child. My mother became irate, and she called me an ungrateful, horrible daughter among other insults.

The next day, I packed my stuff and moved out. As I headed out the door with her continuous insults ringing in my ears, I stopped her and said, "You will no longer control me, and you must stop insulting me if you still want me in your life." I kept my contact with her very limited. I learned that I needed to stay away from her. I realized that being around her was not healthy for me, given her egocentric ways. I still respected my mother as a human being, but at a distance. Years later, during her last few years, I saw in her eyes how she desperately wanted me back in her life. Even though she asked for my forgiveness, and I granted it, I couldn't bring myself to have her in my everyday life. The phrase "Blood is thicker than water" simply did not work for me.

In my salon, I also came across clients with narcissistic behavior, some of whom I will never forget. Some of their comments made me feel that I was far below them. I dreaded the day of their appointment while I bottled in the way they talked to me. I finally had to kindly tell them to find another place for their facials. Today, I love my clients and love going to work. These are my clients, friends, and some family members with whom I have developed great relationships.

Addressing a significant incident with my husband proved to be just as difficult as the other challenges I encountered. Marriage is challenging to begin with—two people with many differences who come together as one to form a family. When I got married, I didn't know how to communicate, and my self-esteem and confidence were low. This enabled my husband to amplify his narcissistic behavior. He was completely oblivious to my feelings. He didn't realize the pain he was causing me and that only distorted my self-esteem and confidence even more. My husband was a very vocal man. He learned from his upbringing that talking and joking about sex and staring at other women were acceptable and harmless behaviors. Meanwhile I was trying to adjust to my new life and accept his behavior as it was tearing me down.

One day, we went on vacation to Cancun with our kids. There were two pools next to each other. The kids were in the pool with the water slides. My husband was at the other pool with the bar. I was going back and forth between the two pools so I could watch my kids. When I came up behind my husband, I noticed he was staring at a girl sitting on the other side of the pool with her legs open. I could hear my husband talking to himself as if he were talking to her. Let's just say it was inappropriate.

After a few minutes the girl started heading in our direction. My husband stood up, expanded his chest like a rooster, and sucked in his stomach. He devoured her with his eyes from head to toe. Standing behind him, I whispered, "You do know you are here with your wife and kids, right?" He deflated like a flat tire. At first I tried to justify his behavior and even laugh about it. After all, he had to go home with me and the kids. But as he followed me to a spot where no one was around, I exploded and called him every name in the book. He was shocked to hear the words I used.

When I headed to our room to take a shower, I cried. I told myself I did not want to be like my mother by using profanity to express what I was feeling, yet I had done just that. I refused to let the incident ruin my kids' vacation. I signed up for every excursion I could to keep us busy and make the time go faster.

After we returned home, my husband and I decided to seek professional help. It was a journey—like navigating a boat on the ocean. At times, the waters were calm, while at other times, the waves threatened to overturn us. Despite the challenges, we persevered, and now we enjoy each other's company more than ever. We both learned valuable lessons. My husband needed to be more sensitive to my feelings, and I had to be less sensitive to certain situations. It wasn't easy for either of us, but we're both glad we went through it together.

There are three strategies that have really helped me grow in dealing with narcissism:

- Recognizing narcissistic behavior
- Setting boundaries
- Communicating effectively

To **recognize narcissistic behavior**, I had to learn the meaning of narcissism and understand how it affected my life. I initially hesitated to categorize people as "narcissists," because of the negative connotation associated with the term. However, I have observed that narcissistic behavior often stems from someone's upbringing and the people around them who never confronted their behavior when they were younger. These people were often treated as if they could do no wrong, leading to a sense of entitlement and self-importance that can manifest as narcissistic behavior.

I **set boundaries** by creating concentric circles:

Circle 1: the few people I fully trust and with whom I can let down my guard

Circle 2: people I see frequently with whom I connect in a formal manner, but still exercise caution with

Circle 3: people with whom I only connect on occasion and keep at a distance

Throughout my life, I have placed people in these circles accordingly. By setting boundaries and letting people know that their behavior is not acceptable, I have been able to prevent it from escalating or becoming more frequent. This has also helped my husband become more empathetic and respectful, and it has fostered a healthier and happier environment.

When I started working on my **communication skills** by simply speaking up, I began to make progress. Speaking up was incredibly difficult and painful for me. I remember my throat tightening and stuttering as I struggled to voice my thoughts. Often, my words made no sense, and I would end up crying with anger. However, I also knew that ignoring someone's narcissistic behavior would only enable them to become more manipulative. So, I kept trying until I got stronger.

When it came to our marriage, both my husband and I were responsible for the situation. I failed to recognize his behavior and speak up in the moment, and he failed to acknowledge or show remorse for his actions. However, parting ways was never an option. We both had to work toward finding a happy medium, even if we would never fully agree with each other. Being married comes with its challenges, but things like spending time with our kids, going on date nights, and traveling together make it all worth it.

The moral of my story is to reach out to those who, like me, struggle with recognizing and expressing their feelings. I hope to inspire anyone who feels trapped in a difficult relationship and encourage them to find strategies to overcome the challenges of speaking up in any situation, whether in their personal or professional life.

For more than twenty-five years, licensed esthetician **Lorena Coello** has helped thousands of clients address their skincare needs to reveal beautiful and more youthful skin. She is the owner and founder of Personalized Skin Care (PSC), a full-service studio and shop offering consultations and advanced skincare treatments, including facials, microblading, micro-needling and more. Through PSC, Lorena has also developed a line of personalized skincare products designed to meet the daily needs of people with all skin types while addressing common concerns like aging, acne, sensitivity, and many others.

Lorena understands that most people are bombarded with images, messages, and ads promoting "the next best thing" in skincare. To save clients from having to sift through confusing information on their own, Lorena forges ongoing relationships that ensure they always have individual, focused assessments of their skin.Armed with this information, Lorena provides recommendations that help guide customers toward products that will optimize their unique skincare regimen.

Lorena's dedication to her work shines through in everything she does. Making others look and feel great has been incredibly rewarding for this self-made professional who entered the industry at just twenty-two years old with no guidance or support. An abuse survivor who left a broken home at age fifteen, Lorena has overcome several difficult challenges along her road to success. Today, she is thrilled to be living her passion for serving a loyal customer base. Of Mexican descent, Lorena is bilingual and proudly offers her services in both Spanish and English.

www.PersonalizedSkincareSolution.com

THE JESUS MINDSET

Lori Giovannini

Do you sometimes feel lonely or not good enough? Is your life missing meaning and purpose? Let me tell you a story.

> Once upon a time, there was a young girl who lived in a messed-up world. Her family, like many, was dysfunctional. She felt unwanted, unworthy, and lonely. She turned to many harmful behaviors and rebelled against the very things that would help her.
>
> One day, after trying everything to fix her own life, she remembered how her grandmother would pray to Jesus when times were tough. *What do I have to lose?* she thought, and she began to talk to Jesus. To her surprise, she felt a love she had never felt before. Could Jesus be her Prince Charming? She wanted to continue to feel that love, and as she drew closer to Him, He led her to the Jesus Mindset.

Jesus wants to be in your great love story, too! He wants to collaborate with those who want Him. He wants to connect directly with you.

Today, as a Professional Brain Health Trainer certified by the Amen Clinics and a Positive Intelligence Coach, I teach my clients to use the spiritual power in their mind. I call it the Jesus Mindset.

The Jesus Mindset is a process in which your mind connects directly with the mind of Jesus. It's the ability to see how Jesus sees. It's discerning your life challenges alongside Jesus, who already knows what's best and how it will work out. It's enjoying a relationship with someone who only wants the best for you. This process changed my life, and with practice, you, too, can learn to quickly tap into the Spirit of Jesus—the Holy Spirit—at any time so you never feel unworthy, unwanted, or lonely.

The truth is that your life is created in your brain. The brain is a complex computer that controls the whole body. It houses the mind and is where your spirit, soul, and Jesus convene. Brain imaging shows that the right side of the brain lights up when you are reading Scripture, praying, and meditating. It's as if we have a Wi-Fi connection to our Creator with a homing device that eventually takes us back to God.

Throughout your lifetime, your brain gathers information and creates beliefs based upon data and conclusions received from your environment. Well-meaning parents, relatives, teachers, church leaders, educational systems, coaches, news, TV, social media, and the internet influence, mold, and shape the thoughts in your belief systems. Those thoughts are stored in your brain cells, and they affect who you are, the way you feel, and how you act. Your actions and behaviors create your results.

This automatic thinking helps your brain be more efficient by cells quickly supplying the way you should think in any situation. This process takes away your ability to think on your own, allowing your mind to feed you thoughts that are not 100 percent true. These lies keep you from becoming the true essence of who God created you to be, and you end up giving your power to brain cells that, in turn, run your daily life. Developing the Jesus Mindset helps you take your power back and allows the power of the Holy Spirit to give you the grace to see what is best in any situation.

God gave us free will; He will never decide your thoughts for you. You must seek His will—what He thinks—by intentionally asking for His wisdom through meditation, prayer, reading scripture and learning about Him. In doing so, you activate the mind of Christ. Satan, on the other hand, can distract you with negative thoughts and lies, but he cannot make you do anything.

You have free will to choose what to think, feel, and act on. Sometimes it's difficult to know who is talking in your mind. Satan's lies seem so real, but believing his lies always leads you down the wrong path. This is another reason that striving toward hearing the discerning mind of Jesus is so important.

Jesus is not the author of the negative thoughts rolling around in your mind, the thoughts that are beating you up and keeping you small. Those quick-thinking brain cells may seem helpful and work for some situations, but automatic thinking can be dangerous. Unfortunately, much of your thinking is done this way, which is why you experience so many negative emotions. Thoughts creating negative emotions should always be discerned. The Jesus Mindset includes a simple process for understanding God's will in any given circumstance. Here is my seven-step discernment process:

1. Find a quiet place where you will not get easily distracted. Breathe deeply and think about something that is going on in your life with which you are struggling. Write your thoughts about it. Writing out the story you are telling yourself can be very mentally and emotionally revealing.

2. Read over what you've written and circle the parts that are 100 percent true. Hint: Facts do not contain an adjective or an emotion. Now, underline all the thoughts you are telling yourself about those facts. Hint: Negative emotions arise from untrue or conflicting thoughts.

3. If only parts of the story are true, decide whether thinking this way is helpful. Will the parts that aren't true serve you in any way and produce the results you desire? If not, ask yourself, "How else can I think about this situation?" Keep asking this question until your brain runs out of ideas. Every solution you write about may not be possible. Still, don't skip this step. It allows you to take back your power from some well-meaning (or not) brain cells.

4. Test out your new ideas or solutions. Give yourself the opportunity to envision doing something different in this situation. Ask yourself, "What would love do?" Get curious."I wonder why I am thinking this way. Which idea do I feel most peaceful with?" Don't judge your ideas; just test them. Write down the idea or ideas you feel most comfortable with.

5. Ask Jesus to come to your assistance in this situation. Spend a moment in prayer and meditation, visualizing Jesus. See Jesus excited to help you. Sit with Jesus or walk with Him as He holds your hand. If you have a tough time with visualization, look at a picture of Jesus and feel the love He has for you. I visualize myself sitting under a shade tree in a beautiful garden with Jesus. I have had many conversations with Jesus this way.

6. Present the idea or solution to Jesus that made you feel most peaceful and pray for the Holy Spirit's wisdom. Jesus loves to protect and guide you. Jesus loves you and wants the best for you. If you present your needs to Jesus, you will feel the peace of God in your decision.

7. Feel confident in the decision and take action. If you don't see positive results right away, know they will come in God's time and in His way! Jesus is in the middle of the situation so the right things are in motion. It may not feel good, but what is best for you and your life has the hand of Jesus on it.

No matter how difficult the circumstance, you and Jesus decide how to think about it. Daily use of the Jesus Mindset gives you a sense of peace. Taking back your thoughts by choosing not to let those automatic brain cells run your show. You have the freedom to intentionally decide the meaning you attach to every situation. Bringing the wisdom of Jesus into your decisions leads you closer to your divine purpose, which gives meaning to your life.

When you take your negative thoughts captive and process them through the Jesus Mindset, you allow your mind to physically shift from the left, more negative, more analytical side of your brain to the right, positive, spiritual side. This shift allows you to see your situation in a true light, with more options, opportunities, and reasons to be grateful.

The Jesus Mindset shows you the true meaning and purpose of your negative circumstances and the reasons why you may be experiencing them. Jesus uses the challenging times of life for growth with new opportunities that can put you on your path to holiness.

Collaborating with Jesus is not automatic; it's a moment of grace. It's a Holy Moment! Using the power of the Holy Spirit in the Jesus Mindset process creates a spiritual awakening that brings peace, joy, and eternal rewards.

Once you get into a habit of going through this discernment process of the Jesus Mindset, you will notice your brain shifting automatically without skipping a beat. It will help you break free from routine negative thought processes and provide new positive perspectives on tough situations. Practicing these seven steps will convert this process into a mindset you will constantly use.

As you live life through the lens of the Jesus Mindset, you will begin to see events unfold differently and experience the clarity and meaning behind life's challenges instead of the stress of reacting to them. These Holy Moments will become amazing blessings along your journey.

Are you ready to learn more about how to let go of your negative thoughts and live more in the Jesus Mindset? Visit my website for your free digital journal.

Lori Giovannini is an international speaker and holistic wellness coach who uses her education and experience as a licensed Professional Brain Health Coach and Trainer certified by the

Amen Clinics, Life and Weight Loss Coach with the Life Coach School, and certified Positive Intelligence Coach.

Lori shows how brain health, science, spirituality, and mindset work together to create a happy, harmonious, and healthy Life. She teaches her clients how to weaken their negative mind chatter and rewire their brain through mental fitness, living without the stress and anxiety of life's circumstances. Lori teaches the Jesus Mindset to help her clients connect to the mind of God for clarity, discernment, and purpose.

Lori has more than twenty years of experience facilitating retreats, seminars, and workshops, including Your Unique Call to Purpose, The Jesus Mindset, You Are Not Stuck with the Brain You Have, Living in Your Temperaments, Your Spiritual Gifts, and The Reason Cycle, along with many talks on brain health and longevity.

Lori and her husband, Lou, live in Redington Beach, Florida. Married for thirty-four years, they have three adult children. Lori likes to read, find the next best health cure, golf, travel, and spend time with her spouse and family.

Lori's mindset techniques, coaching tools, and health tips help anyone at any stage or phase of life. Her mission is to help people live life with love, purpose, passion, and fulfilled faith.

www.JesusMindset.com

POSSIBILITIES INTO REALITY

Cheryl Green

"With man this is impossible, but with God all things are possible."

—Matthew 19:26

Creation is evidence of a Creator, the Founder of origin. He laid the foundations of the earth, created the entire universe, and scooped out the mountains. He painted the sky blue and put the stars in their silvery sockets, too! He is all that. I thought you knew!

Behold the masterpiece now at hand; humanity is the Master's plan. In Adam, God breathed the first family tree and brought forth a spiritual being, and we are His offspring, created in His likeness, conformed to His image (see Genesis 1:26).

The order and care God showed in the six workdays of creation tells us that He always had one purpose in mind. God divided His workweek into two groups of days. For three days, He gave order to the formless earth. Then, for three days, He filled the formed but empty earth. Day by day, God purposely ordered His work until it reached its climax on the sixth day. That's when He created humanity, for whose benefit the whole earth was created. God's creation of humanity is the high point of His six days of creative work regarding Planet Earth. All that God created within the first five days points to one divine purpose. God's plan was always to create a being "in His own image," capable of communicating with Him and for whom He has an ultimate plan in relation to the universe. In creating us, He knew no bounds. We are His ultimate creation, His greatest miracle. We are complete living beings able to adjust to any climate, hardship, or challenge, and we are able to manage our destiny without any interference from Him. With the right atmosphere, vegetation, and living creatures surrounding Him, all was ready for God's final creation: humanity. God prepared the environment as carefully as any parent prepares the nursery for the expected firstborn son or daughter.

God ordained and arranged that we would rule the world and have dominion. That is a fact, not religion or opinion. He gave us the breath of life, paradise, and personhood. At last, He blessed and confessed, "It is all good." He endowed us with Godlike power unknown to any other creatures. He calls us his own. Loves us to the bone. Our worth we cannot measure. Our success is His pleasure. Every good gift is from above. God loves us with an everlasting love. Christ loved us and gave Himself up for us. There is no greater love than this, that a man lay down his life for us (see John 15:13). He was hung up for our hang-ups. He went through unspeakable abuse. He was marred, disfigured, and severely injured, suffering both physical and spiritual pain. He took on our sicknesses and diseases; "He was wounded for our transgressions, bruised for our iniquities" (Isaiah 53:5-8), and He bled until he ran out of blood to bring us peace and victory. There are no shortages in God. There are no limitations in God. He does not recognize recessions, downturns, calamities, depressions, famines, natural disasters, or hurricanes. Neither is He bound to these. He is the God of the supernatural. Creation declares His glory, and the universe displays His Majesty (see Psalm 19:1).

Almighty God, the Creator, had a Son, but He wanted a family, so He created us in His image so He could relate to us and we could know Him intimately. He gives us the BIBLE (Basic Instructions Before Leaving Earth) so we may know Him. God created people for a loving relationship with Him. We are the

DNA of Christ. There is nothing you can dream up that your mind does not know exactly how to bring about. I declare that you are special and extraordinary. You are above average. You have been custom made. You are one-of-a-kind. Of all the things God created, what He is most proud of is not the solar system, not the sunset, not the amazing animals. The creation that God calls His masterpiece (see Ephesians 2:10) is you. You are His most prized possession. He created you in His very image. We are offspring, and we all have dreams God has put in our hearts, visions we want to accomplish. The Bible says that without a vision, people perish (see Proverbs 29:18). If we do not have a vision, then we will create the life we have always known.

What is a vision? A vision is a mental image, picture, or revelation of your future state. Physical creations follow mental ideas and images. To make your deepest desires a reality, you first need to be clear about what you want and hold that image in your mind. Your vision is a bridge that will take you from your present into your future. God speaks to us out of our destiny, not our present condition. If you can see it, you can have it, but you cannot have it if you cannot see it. We walk by faith, not by sight (see 2 Corinthians 5:7). Those who cannot see the invisible cannot do the impossible.

Do you remember when we were kids and no dream seemed too big? Our imagination was unlimited! Every one of us, when we were young, had a common trait—we were dreamers. As we get older, doubt creeps in, and those vivid dreams begin to fade. Maybe we tried to reach several goals but were never successful. People began to tell us that we could not do the things we wanted. Those things were impossible. Responsible people do not pursue their dreams. Settle down. Get a job. Be dependable. Take care of business. Live mundane. Be content.

Who stole your dream? Was it your parents? The voices of your past telling you that you could not do it? Was it a teacher? A voice that called you stupid? What made you quit? Was it fear?

The Good News is that you can learn to dream again and turn your possibilities into reality.

What do you really, really want? Once you decide what you want, **nothing can stand in your way!**

Three Steps to Turn Possibilities into Reality

1. **Dream Big**—Begin with the end in mind, clarify your TARGET, and write a detailed description. Everything has its origin in the mind. Your imagination is the preview of the coming attraction. God has given us the power to shape our world by our thoughts. Thoughts are agents of creation. Your cumulative thoughts have brought you to where you are today. If you do not change your direction, you will end up where you are heading. The first principle in any God-given dream is that the dream should be so big that there is no way you can do it being the person you are today. The real purpose behind God-given dreams is to get you to grow. If you can achieve your dream being the person you are right now, then the dream is too small. If your dream doesn't require you to get up at a different time in the morning, hang around different people, read different books, watch videos, and listen to podcasts, make changes in your habits, changes in your lifestyle, changes in your values, changes in your goals, changes in what you do from day-to-day, and changes in the way you make decisions, then it's not big enough.

2. **Make a Plan**—Have a clear vision of where you want to end up and, like a GPS, start designing a path between the two points to get you there. Remember, roadblocks are not stop signs; they are qualifiers. Set a ninety-day timeline to achieve your goal or reach a particular milestone. The pressure of a timeline will create flow, profound creativity, and a sense of urgency.

3. **Move Forward Every Day.** Start, take action, and never stop. Commit to doing something (even if it is small) that moves you toward your goal every day.

For more than fifteen years, **Cheryl Green** has helped people all around the world, from all walks of life and of all ages, clarify their dreams and bring them to life. As a Certified Dream-Builder coach, Cheryl Green can help you design and manifest a life that's in harmony with your Soul's purpose. With the DREAM-BUILDER transformational tools, proven system, and loving support, Cheryl's clients have authored books, started businesses, purchased their dream homes, attracted loving partners, found more meaningful jobs, and overcome all manner of "impossible" circumstances to create lives they absolutely love living. As a sought-after expert on the "Invisible Side of Success," Cheryl guides her clients through a powerful transformational system developed by elite teachers in the personal development world. Through their books, live events, masterminds, and online programs, she helps people worldwide achieve new heights of spiritual aliveness, financial prosperity, and authentic success.

No matter what you have experienced in the past, or what you are going through right now, Cheryl is available to share her knowledge and guide you toward the achievement of your dreams. With Cheryl's help, you too can learn how to harness the incredible power that lies within you, and radically change your life for the better—in far less time, and with far less effort than you might believe is possible right now. With her help, you can become a "Brave Thinker," a "Dream Builder" . . . and create a life you absolutely *love* living!

https://linktr.ee/CherylGreenRhaps

FROM LIMITATION TO LIBERATION

Miranda Kaur

This chapter is dedicated to every individual who does not fit into the mold of the ideal standards defined by society; who does not meet their cultural and or family expectations; or who has felt different from others, be it due to ethnicity, religious beliefs, skin color, weight challenges, sexual orientation, etc.

Hong Kong, December 1997. Savoring the last bite of my buttered toast, I decided to finish my breakfast out on the balcony. I stepped out with my mug of hot Indian tea and leaned against the balcony railing. Shielding my eyes from the morning light, I surveyed the neighborhood.

It was a fine, warm day. The smell of freshly cut grass permeated the air. A big, black bee was buzzing around, flying in a pattern of eight. It was too close for comfort. I was about to make a mad dash back inside when it changed course and flew away. *Phew!*

The silence was broken by the deafening sound of my neighbor's dogs barking. The ear-piercing sound of car horns and the screeching of tires added to the cacophony of noise.

As I gazed at the horizon, I became cognizant that the noise in the outer landscape was mirroring the noise in my inner landscape. I had denied it for some months now, but I was disillusioned, confused, and unhappy. I had avoided addressing this, hoping it would go away like magic. It was becoming crystal clear that wasn't about to happen. I couldn't suppress it any longer.

My leisurely breakfast had been a luxury, a departure from my previously frenetic lifestyle. I had been a flight attendant with Cathay Pacific Airways for several years. It had been an exciting and dream position. It had offered a myriad of experiences—I had traveled the world over, met a wide variety of people, and learned about different cultures. But the time had come; I was ready to hang up my wings. I was ready for a new chapter in my life. I was looking forward to no longer having to spend the holidays away from home, miss family events, or battle jet lag.

So, I took the option for early retirement, and it had come into effect seven months ago. I had eagerly looked forward to my post-retirement life. The lie-ins, the leisurely mealtimes, the gentler pace of life.

As the initial euphoria wore off, however, the pendulum swung to the opposite end. I began to feel a deep sense of loss. My personal and professional lives had been intertwined, and they had revolved around the airline industry. The airline had been my community, my family, my tribe. My career and title had defined me, and with that gone now, I was feeling rootless. I didn't know who I was or what I was about. I needed answers, desperately.

Pushing through the hazy malaise that engulfed me, I began to explore personal transformation workshops. This was something that had intrigued me for many years, but I had only ever dipped my toes in previously. It was the beginning of a fifteen-year quest as I immersed myself in the self-discovery process.

Growing up in Singapore, I had struggled with my self-identity from my earliest years. As a subset of an ethnic minority group (a Sikh within the Indian diaspora, to be exact), I couldn't find any role models I could identify with, and I couldn't relate to any of the images and story lines presented in the media. Inclusive and diversity marketing were not de rigueur back in the sixties and seventies.

Additionally, I experienced numerous incidents of racial microaggressions. Cumulatively, these had a deleterious effect on my fragile sense of belonging. I vividly remember an incident where I was told, "You smell really nice—for an Indian." Then there were the constant disparaging comments about the Indian culture, from the strong aroma of curry to the application of coconut oil on our hair to our mannerisms. The casual use of derogatory terms and the mocking of the Indian accent was not unusual either. Each incident was soul-destroying.

As a result, I grew up thinking that being different was not acceptable, that it was not a good thing. All I wanted was to fit in and be accepted by my peers. I'm ashamed to say, I distanced myself from my culture. Inevitably, there was a void in my self-identity, one that would come to be filled with an inauthentic narrative.

The feeling of being inadequate followed me into my young adulthood. It led me to make poor lifestyle choices, get involved in unhealthy relationships, and suppress my voice. The consequences were always disastrous.

Through my self-discovery journey, I learned that the first step to move forward began with fully accepting myself. This was the essential foundational step—one that would support, nourish, and balance me during turbulent times.

I learned that the combination of our dark aspects (our quirks, foibles, and flaws) and our light aspects is what makes us unique individuals. Every individual has distinct physical, emotional, and mental attributes—from our body sizes to our skin tones, our emotional temperaments to our personality traits, our intellect to our creative skills. These diversities are the hues and shades of color that add richness to the tapestry of our life, radiating out from our personal world to the global world.

We have to appreciate that being different is exactly what we bring to the table. We contribute to the world, not by imitating someone else's personality or traits, but by our own unique aspects.

When I finally began to embrace all parts of myself and reacquainted myself with my heritage, I found myself free from the shackles of limitations. My voice roared back to life, my heart was filled with joy, and my soul soared to new heights.

The skills and strategies I learned from my personal transformation journey cut through my inner turmoil and shed a light on the way forward, giving me clarity, direction, and hope. I emerged on the other side fully owning myself and with unwavering confidence.

I am now privileged to be able to support others on their self-discovery journeys, and it brings me immense joy when I witness their transformations as they lose their limitations and discover true liberation.

I hope my journey has inspired you to take your first step toward building your foundation, too, so you can be yourself and thrive!

Miranda Kaur is a speaker and transformational trainer. Since 2007, Miranda has been helping individuals and professionals to turn their lives around by transforming their disempowering beliefs into empowering beliefs. This has helped them to take back control of their lives and achieve their desired goals.

Miranda brings to the table a forty-year career that spanned the entertainment, airline, and personal transformation industries. Her stint as a flight attendant with Cathay Pacific Airways offered her the opportunity to travel the world and connect with a diverse range of people and cultures. Her interactions with the thousands of people gave her unparalleled insights into the human psyche.

On a personal level, Miranda experienced a series of major life events over a thirteen-year period—from an acrimonious divorce and multiple home relocations to being the primary caregiver for a parent with dementia, the loss of loved ones, and the profound grieving process that followed.

Leveraging her career and lived experiences, Miranda compiled all that she had learned and experienced and distilled it into her secret weapon: **The 7 Keys**. A natural empath and intuitive, she incorporates these modalities into her training programs whenever appropriate. Miranda's ultimate mission is to help others move from denial to acceptance, from pain to joy, and from limitation to liberation.

https://www.mirandakaur.com

DO YOU HAVE A BOLD SPIRIT?

Dr. Susie Mierzwik

As I was walking across the parking lot in a shopping center recently, I overheard two people speaking about church. I joined in the conversation and asked them where they both attended. After listening to their individual responses, I invited them to attend Easter service at my church. I wished them a good day and turned to leave. One of the ladies replied, "Wow, you have a bold spirit!"

That response surprised me, and it got me thinking about how acting boldly has had a considerable effect on my life in many ways.

It reminded me of when I was in college and had just been accepted to a junior- year exchange program in Chico, California. I had never heard of this place, since I lived in suburban New Jersey. But I was looking for wider horizons than those in my little town of sixteen thousand people. I told my mom that I would be jumping out of airplanes and climbing mountains in my future. While I have yet to leap out of an airplane, this bold attitude has opened many doors in my life.

When I was twenty-two years old and newly arrived in Virginia Beach, I got myself a job selling encyclopedias door-to-door. It seems hilarious to think about this today when most people don't even know what an encyclopedia IS, let alone lug one around in a giant briefcase throughout the neighborhood looking for buyers! Yet this was a job I held at the time, and I even made a sale!My attitude was simply, "Why not?"

Next I worked for a credit company, locating buyers who had defaulted on their car loan. My boss, who worked for the bank, simply went out at night and repossessed the car until they made good on the loan payments. There was a certain thrill involved in tracking down someone who had tried to hide. I had to be bold in asking questions and getting clues to the whereabouts of the vehicle in default.

The next bold action I took became the start of my long career in education. I had applied for a teaching job, but I hadn't heard anything by late August. So I hopped into the car and headed down to the school where I really wanted to work. I was armed with four trusty props, a spelling book, a dictionary, a pencil, and a pair of glasses, so I would look like a teacher. I walked boldly into the front office and announced that I was there to see the principal. The secretary informed me that he was not available. "No problem," I said, and I sat down, prepared to wait. Two long hours later, the door to his office creaked open. I popped up and introduced myself. I told him I hadn't received a reply to my teaching application, and I knew school was starting next week. I asked if I could walk around campus, familiarize myself, and set up my classroom. Without waiting for his reply, I marched out of the office and strolled around the campus like I belonged there. I was sure I wouldn't see the inside of that school again. But the following morning I received a phone call, and I was hired!

Next, I faced the problem of getting to the school each day, since my husband and I owned only one car. I was able to convince the pastor at my church to let me be the bus driver for the high school students attending the school where I would be teaching. Every day, I had to take off my "bus driver" hat, so to speak, and put on my "teacher hat."In every instance of my career, my strategy was always to get the job first, and then figure it out later.

When I began my teaching career at the age of twenty-three, I was only a few years older than my high school students. My boldness in snagging the position was followed by several months of quaking in my proverbial boots, as I learned my job.

During my third year of teaching, I enrolled in an MBA program. My fellow students were all career military officers, and I hadn't even taken any basic business courses yet. However, I was somewhat accustomed to jumping into new situations without fear, so I enrolled and learned along the way.

A couple years later I discovered that my manager-in-training position was being eliminated, so I asked to speak to the vice president of finance, the head of my division. I wanted to hear the real story. She told me simply that my boss didn't like me. She said, "If your boss doesn't like you, you have to go!" That made sense to me. Instead of dressing up my layoff in terms that disguised reality, I had the courage to seek the truth. I accepted it and moved on.

Four years later, I had to evaluate my current position in the finance department of another large corporation. I decided to be bold and went to a career counselor to find out if I was in the correct field for my personality and interests. Surprisingly, all the data pointed to a career in teaching or sales! I thought my future lay in the corporate finance sector because I had my MBA. So I made another bold move and left corporate America for the quite different path of teaching little people.

Since I enjoyed numbers when they pertained directly to individuals, I continued my side gig with a home-based income tax practice. I enjoyed that for twenty years until mandatory computerization made it impractical.

I began my elementary teaching career by teaching a combination first grade/kindergarten class. That was certainly a lot different than my former job teaching high school English. And it was way different from crunching numbers in corporate finance. However, I was like Brer Rabbit when he was thrown into the briar patch. Bingo! I was in my element. Within the first few weeks, my new principal asked me to give her feedback on the first grade students in my class. She wanted to know if my first graders had been adequately prepared by their former kindergarten teacher. I told her that frankly their last year of school was woefully lacking because it had not equipped them for the requirements of first grade.

The outcome of that bold statement to my new principal was incredible! The next year she appointed me to become the grade level leader for all the kindergarten classes and drastically upgrade the curriculum. Subsequently, our kindergarten students were now taught to read and write sentences, which resulted in their successful promotion to first grade the following year.

I was awarded the Teacher of the Year in 2000, and I had the opportunity to supervise many student teachers during my twenty-year career. I was also able to mentor several parent helpers who later became teachers themselves.

Being bold can have a downside as well, however. I discovered this during my final year of teaching. During my last year, a young, inexperienced new principal landed in my school, and she asked me to violate the union rules by working additional hours outside of our contract without compensation.

Now, working long hours for the benefit of my students was something I had done joyfully throughout my teaching career. I regularly put in hundreds of hours of my own private time every year to plan and prepare for my students. However, what my principal asked me to do was outside the scope of my hours, before school started, so I said no. Her response was to remove me from my leadership position and hand over the reins to two brand new teachers who were still on probation!

That year was a very painful time for me, as I remembered the advice of my former VP of Finance twenty years earlier. I clearly recognized that my current boss disliked me and had effectively cut off my influence.

I decided to take the Golden Handshake that was offered to me. Although it was shrouded in sadness by the way I was tossed aside, I was prepared to move, and I started to consider my next career move.

I had experienced dramatic physical healing for my chronic arthritis pain by using the phototherapy Lifewave patches. Once again I made a bold move and decided to begin my Lifewave business. My target client was a person seeking pain relief without the use of any drugs or chemicals.

I started with people in my business networks. During the COVID-19 pandemic, I began doing my business over Zoom. Now I could reach people everywhere, including Egypt, Tanzania, and the Philippines. The stem cell regeneration patches opened up my market, and now it was worldwide! With our residual income, we began purchasing rental properties, which gave us another stream of income.

Stepping out in boldness has led to greater accomplishments than I could ever have dreamed of reaching!

Dr. Susie Mierzwik retired from teaching after twenty-six years. She has BA in English from Montclair State University, an MBA from Golden Gate University, and an honorary doctorate of humanitarianism from the Global International Alliance in London, UK. Other awards include Teacher of the Year (2000), Women of Distinction (2014), SIMAGlobal Award (2022), and several volunteering awards from the US Senate and US president.

Susie has been an entrepreneur since 2009. She helps clients eliminate pain without drugs using a patented form of phototherapy. There are many applications for this technology, including nondrug pain relief, stem cell regeneration, natural sleep, and more. She is also an author, speaker, and empowerment facilitator.

In 2022, Susie collaborated in three books: *Love Your Haters*, *The Impact of One Voice*,and *100Successful Women Around the World*. She also self-published her memoir *Sow in Tears, Reap in Joy: A Transformational Journey*. She shows her readers three strategies to navigate life when it gets derailed. In 2023, Susie collaborated in five books: *Maintain a Solid Mental Health, It's All About Showing Up. The Impact of Once Voice, Vol. II* and two other titles coming in the Fall of 2023.

Susie and her husband actively volunteer with Samaritan's Purse, an international organization that provides global relief for families and children in crisis. They volunteer in the distribution center to send necessities to needy children across the world.

Visit Susie's website to learn more about stem cell regeneration with phototherapy patches, empowerment groups, and speaking opportunities.

www.SusieMierzwik.com

WHAT YOU DO DEFINES WHO YOU BECOME

Jennifer Marie Pelfini

My husband Michael and I were elated to confirm that we were pregnant—a dream come true! It was June 2017 and in a few weeks I'd be forty-eight years old. Up until meeting my husband, my only dream was career, driven by "do more, be more." Our fertility doctor told us I needed to avoid stress, as I had previously experienced three miscarriages. I laughed out loud when he said this, because my marketing job required a lot of travel, was high visibility, and came with a lot of pressure.

As I headed into the office a week later, I thought, *I work for a good company, I'm newly married, and now we are pregnant. What could be better?* Quietly excited, I walked into a conference room for a meeting. The room was empty. A few minutes later, my supervisor walked in with a notebook and envelope in hand. She told me I was being laid off. My mind was racing as I only partially listened to what my time left at the company would look like. As she continued to explain, I drifted off thinking, *What am I going to do now? I'm pregnant! This is supposed to be my happy time!* I signed the document, left the room, quickly gathered my desk things, and walked out of the building. I was in a daze. This was not my plan.

In shock, I called and left Michael a message letting him know I'd be home early. The layoff left me with feelings of confusion and failure. As a mom-to-be, I knew the rules would be different now—because who would hire a pregnant woman?

As I drove home, I replayed the last year in my head. Michael and I had gotten engaged on a July vacation in Portugal. We decided to marry a few months later, as we saw no reason to wait. As we finalized our small ceremony, we found out his mom needed a critical heart surgery, just three days before our September wedding. She needed a second surgery three days after we married.

We moved in with her to ensure we were available, thinking she'd improve. But the doctors told us there were no more medical cures for her heart. We were at her bedside when she passed on Thanksgiving. It was a painful time for us, not only because of the loss of my newly formed relationship with my mother-in-law, but also the heartbreak that Michael as an only child faced in losing her. Work was relentless, and there was no time off to grieve. For the first time in my life, my family was more important than my career.

Michael saw the look of devastation on my face when I got home. He embraced me and reassured me that everything would be OK. He encouraged me to stay at home while pregnant. There was a lot to do, especially since my family was in Ohio and Florida, and Michael and I were alone together.

Our small Silicon Valley home was made for two single professionals, so we submitted plans to renovate. We thought the work would be complete before our child's birth, but we weren't even in the queue for approvals mid-pregnancy.

We began to visualize what kind of life we wanted for our family. A fast-paced life was no longer a fit. During our last pre-baby vacation, we met a realtor who introduced us to the idea of Reno, Nevada. In a matter of two visits, he found us our dream home right before the new year.

Our daughter, Audriana, was born at the end of January, and when she was six weeks old, we road-tripped to Reno to close on our house. We chose an early summer moving date. We decided to change everything about our lives, including leaving corporate life behind.

We moved to Reno with no plan—we just did it! I leapt into our new life. I breastfed Audriana for the first six months and did all the things a new mom does. My life went from leading projects for the latest technology to being an extension of another person. Determined to nail being a new mom, I sought out moms groups. When some days were overwhelming, I gently reminded myself that this was my dream.

With Audriana as my focus, I completely lost sight of me. I found it difficult to make time for a shower or to brush my hair. My body and mind had completely adjusted around this transition to motherhood. On Audriana's first birthday, I recorded a video, and it was the first time since her birth that I was able to think clearly and construct a full sentence.

Now that Audriana was one, I thought about getting a job. The lure and salary of corporate life was like a drug. I believed I needed it to validate who I was. But every time I interviewed for a job, I'd feel sick. I knew I had no boundaries. While my corporate life had been laden with benefits, privileges, travel, and education, there was a high price to pay for it. I allowed my life to be owned by my career. Now I had my family to think about. The environment I was used to was no place for the mom I wanted to be. Most people thought the technology industry was glamorous, but they didn't see the nonstop emails, constant interruptions, and the inability to ever shut off. I knew I had to find something different.

When the pandemic hit, Audriana was just over two years old, and I was emotionally drained as a stay-at-home mom. We didn't go anywhere, and that meant I was cooking every day. One day I was invited to attend an online kitchen party to shop with Pampered Chef.

While participating in the party, I became inspired. I love the kitchen and cooking and I already had a cooking blog. Direct sales seemed to support my goals with my family. *Maybe I could make this a new business*, I thought. But back in my corporate career, a hiring manager once told me I'd never be able to sell anything because I never carried a bag. I had let myself believe him.

I couldn't stop thinking about this opportunity, though. I was nervous and excited. After waking up five mornings in a row hearing "This is for you," I placed my faith in God's message and signed up to be an independent consultant. Day by day, I built a book of business. With Audriana by my side, I poured all of my passion into doing something I believed I could do. I built a team and achieved awards. I earned all the things I could ever dream of for our kitchen and had an income while doing it. I looked for partnerships and built relationships. I established value propositions and shared experiences. I was authentically real. I was the person I chose to become with great honor. I established myself as my own brand and banked on me. God's way was shining a light on my purpose.

Later that year, delivering an order to our realtor, we both quickly recognized our complimentary marketing skills. I was ready to step out into marketing work again, and he needed marketing support. To start, I would assist with communications for the church diocese—primarily developing and editing content for a Catholic magazine delivered to twenty thousand area homes. Our business relationship grew from there. Excited to rekindle my marketing business, I also began to network in the local community and met other incredible entrepreneurial women.

Through loss, building, and resurfacing, I acquired clarity about what I wanted to do and who I wanted to become. I always had a choice; I just never believed it. This is Jenn Marie Living—the brand I built *is* me.

I didn't do this all by myself. I was fortunate to have a few strong mentors in my life. I like to call them my own personal board of directors. I chose these women because they were honest, supportive, and encouraging in my career and during my transformation.

Women need other women in their corner—women who care enough to push and believe in their dreams. Because of my journey, I became the woman who encourages women and young girls. When you are told, "No, you can't do that," I believe you can. I want to be on your cheering squad, because only you know your full potential given by God. What you do defines who you become, but you have to make that choice to realize it. Only *you* get to decide.

I'm at the beginning of my story. The chapters forward will be true to the vision of my soul, the way God intended. I am providing Audriana with the greatest example of achievement I can provide—to be real. She is watching.

I dedicate this to my sister Bridget, who was on my original board of directors. She joined God in heaven in 2022.

Jennifer Marie Pelfini was born and raised in northeast Ohio and is the oldest of five children. She has a bachelor of science degree from Eastern Michigan University and a master's degree in business administration from Arizona State University, WP Carey School of Business.

After relocating to California during the height of the dot.com era, she spent the majority of her corporate career in marketing, supporting high-tech companies. When she became pregnant at the age of forty-seven, she took the path of motherhood and became a full-time stay at home mom for three years. After this reset, she transformed how she viewed her life and career.

Now she engages with marketing projects and businesses that fuel her passion to make an impact. She hopes to inspire young girls and women in business to be who they desire to be, not who they are told they should be. As a marketing professional, her work focuses on messaging, branding, communications, and strategy.

She lives in Reno, Nevada, with her husband, Michael, and daughter, Audriana. Jennifer is active in the local business community and her church diocese. She and her family enjoy all the blessings the Sierra region has to offer. She loves to cook and create, whether she is experimenting with a new dish to share or crafting a story. She enjoys travel and has been to many countries and cities in her corporate and personal life, but now she enjoys travel most when vacationing with her family.

www.JennMarieLiving.com

BIGGER THAN GRIEF

Arvee Robinson

"Wake up!" I yelled at my sleeping husband. "Wake up!" It was a beautiful Monday morning in October. I had gotten up an hour earlier and quietly walked into the living room to workout. My husband had trouble sleeping and often slept in late. As I was twisting on my SimplyFit board, a feeling came over me: Something was wrong. I quickly dashed into the bedroom, opened the curtains, and cheerfully said to my husband,"Rise and shine." He didn't move. I gently pushed his arm and said, "Wake up, sleepyhead." He didn't move. My heart sank. I began to hit him hard on the arm. "Wake up! Wake up! Don't do this to me," I screamed. I knew at that moment he was gone. The love of my life, my best friend, my husband, Michael, was dead.

A fountain of tears rolled down my cheeks. For a split second, I lost my mind. I didn't know what to do, so I called a friend—no answer. A still, small voice cut through my screaming, and said, "Call 911." What happened next is still a blur. The police came; then the paramedics came. They worked on Michael, but it was too late. Later that day, he was hauled out on a stretcher in a body bag. It happened so fast. During the night, Michael's heart had stopped beating. In the morning, I was left to pick up the pieces of my own broken heart.

Ten years earlier, Michael had been diagnosed with congestive heart failure. He'd been in and out of the hospital, on multiple medications, and had difficulty breathing and walking. And yet, he had a positive attitude, loved people, and never complained. He was a saint. Even though his heart was physically weak, his loving heart was strong.

Six weeks later, he was honored with a Catholic Church service, buried in a neighborhood cemetery, and his life was celebrated by friends and family. I remember people coming up to me and saying, "He's in a better place." I wanted to scream, "*This was a pretty damn good place right here with me!*" Soon after the funeral, the flowers stopped coming, the lunch invitations ceased, the phone calls lessened, and I felt alone for the first time in our twenty years together. Alone with my grief.

"God, please take me home to be with my husband," I would pray. Often, I would imagine running out into the busy street on which I lived. I would tell myself, *It's not suicide if it is an accident.* Every night I cried myself to sleep, and I cried every morning when I realized this new reality was not a dream.

My grief was beginning to consume my life. For months, I canceled appointments, quit networking groups, and worked as little as possible. I attended Grief Share, church meetings, and grief empowerment sessions in the hope to get better and find some relief from the enormous pain and emptiness left in my heart. Nothing seemed to work. I became more and more depressed and isolated.

To make matters worse, six months later, my little boxer dog, Zoee, died unexpectedly from a brain aneurism. A few months later, I had to put her brother, Zeus, down due to cancer spreading throughout his body. I cried out in pain. "Enough!" I yelled at God. "You've taken every living creature out of my life! What am I supposed to do now?" I felt betrayed. Angry. I was alone.

One evening, to pass the time, I was watching YouTube. I came across the most amazing-looking woman, Ernestine Shepherd. She was strong, vibrant, and confident. At eighty-five years old, she is a body builder motivating others to start exercising. Something lit up inside of me. For the first time in months, I felt a flash of excitement and hope. I've exercised all my life, but this was different. I've run two full marathons and five half marathons, hired private trainers, and worked out two or three times per week for years. I didn't look anything close to the way Ernestine looked, and I wanted that badly! I'd heard that exercise releases endorphins and endorphins can help eliminate depression. Lord knows, I needed a ton of them! I said to myself, "This is it! This is the way I can manage my grief."

The next day, I began my journey toward ultimate fitness. Somehow, though, that alone didn't seem like enough. I needed to set a goal that was *bigger than my grief.* A goal that was so big that it scared me. A goal so big that I couldn't think of any else, and yet a goal that was attainable. After only a few moments, I decided I was going to compete in a bodybuilding contest in two years at the age of seventy, like Ernestine had.

First, I watched YouTube videos and worked out at home. Next, I hired a fitness coach from Canada and used her online program for three months. I quickly outgrew that program and began searching for more. I knew I needed an in-person trainer to train me properly to lift weights and prepare me for competition. "Where am I going to find that kind of trainer?" I asked myself.

God answers the prayers and desires of the heart. One day, He showed me the perfect place, Addicted to Fitness, a private gym dedicated to weight training and preparing individuals for competition. And it was only fifteen minutes from my house! I saw their ad and phone number on Facebook, and I immediately picked up the phone and called. The owner, Arlene Cherry, answered the phone. I explained what I wanted to do, and then I told her, "But I'm sixty-eight years old."

Quickly, she chimed back, "I'm sixty!"

In that moment, I knew I had called the right place. I signed up for private and group sessions and committed to working out four days a week.

That was months ago. Today, I work out six days a week. I have lost weight, toned up, and become an inspiration to others. Soon I will compete in a bodybuilding bikini contest. More importantly, I find that I am able to manage my grief, eliminate depression, live a healthy lifestyle, and look forward to the future. No, it's not perfect, and I am still navigating the single widow life, but it's a lot easier when you have something to focus on that's bigger than yourself and your grief.

Handling grief is an individual process. Some people manage their grief quickly, while for others, it can take many years. The solutions that work are different for everyone. There are no magic processes, activities, or timelines.

While you may be navigating your way through what seems to be a long, dark, never-ending tunnel, let me share with you some ideas that could light your way.

Using the acronym GRIEF, I'm going to share five steps you can take toward managing and even lessening the overwhelming feelings of sadness.

G stands for Goal. Set a huge goal for yourself. A goal that is so big that you and everyone around you will know when you've reached it. A goal that will stretch you in new ways. Something that is challenging and will make you feel uncomfortable at first— yet a goal that excites you and makes you come alive at the mere thought of it.

R stands for Right. Make sure your goal and the timing of accomplishing that goal is *right* for you. This is neither a race nor a competition. This is your journey to make alone— your journey to healing from grief.

I stands for Inspired. Set a goal that inspires you to take massive action. A goal that you desire so much that it propels you out of bed every morning. Something that you desire to do more than anything else. A goal that gives you unwavering joy.

E stands for Evolutionary. Select a goal that will transform you from the person you are today, full of grief, into who you want to become: a person who is free of sadness, pain, and misery.

F stands for Focus. Keep your eyes on your goal. Only share it with people who will support you. Remember, this goal is for you, no one else. You don't need other people's approval or their blessings, only your own.

Grief comes from many different situations in life: a lost loved one, a lost career, a divorce, and many other life-altering circumstances. You may never completely get rid of it. However, you can manage it by using these five simple techniques. By doing so, you will find that one day, you are bigger than your own grief.

Arvee Robinson, The Master Speaker Trainer, international keynote speaker, and three-time bestselling author, captivates her audiences with high-energy, high-content, interactive presentations filled with vivid stories. Her audiences have fun while learning workable strategies they can put into action immediately. Arvee has presented more than fifty-five hundred motivational keynotes and content-rich educational programs all over the world. She has shared the stage with speaking giants Mark Victor Hansen, Brian Tracy, Les Brown, Sharon Lechter, Loral Langemeier, Tom Hopkins, and many others.

As an in-demand speaking coach for two decades, Arvee has taught more than seventy-three thousand business owners how to attract more clients, generate unlimited leads, and grow their businesses fast by clearly communicating what they do. She teaches simple, proven systems for delivering persuasive presentations, magnetic introductions, five-minute business showcases, and compelling promotional videos. Arvee has helped hundreds of individuals eliminate nervousness, command their audiences' attention, and deliver sales-winning speeches.

Arvee is a published author of *Speak Up Get Clients: How to Use Public Speaking as a Marketing Strategy to Attract High-Paying Clients*. She has published chapters in five collaborative books, number-one bestseller *The Impact of One Voice*, Volume

I, number-one bestseller *Live the Life You Love,* number-one bestseller *Ready Aim Captivate, Inspiration to Realization, and Profitable Social Media.* She is also the host of the *Million Dollar Speaker Podcast.*

On a personal note, Arvee holds a BS degree in Information Systems, has achieved many outstanding awards and trophies, and lives in Southern California.

www.ArveeRobinson.com

FOCUS ON WHAT MATTERS: DON'T SETTLE—YOU DESERVE MORE!

Katrina Sawa

Eighteen years ago, I realized I was settling. I was settling for a relationship that wasn't loving, passionate, affectionate, and/or supportive. I'd been married to my *starter husband* for six years, and around that time, I decided to start my own business. I thought my husband would be supportive because we met doing outside sales, and you have to be pretty outgoing and ballsy to do that. But I was mistaken.

Once he began getting regular monthly paychecks from his "real job," that he started nine months after we met, he got very comfortable. I, on the other hand, still had the desire to start my own business, which I did. It was a marketing consulting company, and to get clients I began networking locally. Soon I realized that I was good at this!

I was passionate about helping other business owners make money and grow their business. I was really excited about my career for the first time in my life. And although I'd been in sales and marketing jobs all my life, I knew I didn't know what I didn't know as far as running my own business. I sought out local workshops, coaches, and mentors who were more experienced.

One day a friend suggested that I travel to Los Angeles to attend an online marketing workshop. The cost was three thousand dollars plus travel and hotel. I didn't have the money to invest in that, but she was adamant that this would change my life. I went to my husband and told him I needed to do this and would have to put it on a credit card. He said I should make the money first, and then I could afford to do it without debt. (To this day, this is the biggest challenge my clients face with their own spouses.) But I knew better, and I did it anyway.

What I learned at this workshop changed my life! The people I met there were so passionate and driven. I was on a high just hanging around them for four days. I knew that I had to stay in this energy to keep the momentum going and continue getting support to grow my business, and in order to do that, my next step was to join the mastermind hosted by the leader of the workshop. The mastermind was fifteen thousand dollars. I couldn't afford that, either, but I decided to jump in anyway without first asking my husband. I was trusting myself that I could and would make some big changes quickly.

Within the first ninety days of working with that mentor, I ramped up my business to a decent level of revenue and with a different type of business model, one where I wasn't working by the hour for people anymore. I positioned myself more as a consultant, and my clients paid me to tell them what to do instead of me doing it for them!

Unfortunately, my husband and I grew further apart. I remember one day going to a local networking event where a few people asked me how I was doing. My answer was "I'm great! I'm fine!" with a big smile. But I wasn't fine. That night and almost every night after that for a year, I cried myself to sleep. No longer were my husband and I connected, affectionate, loving, or even kind to each other. I realized I was settling for someone who wasn't going to change and wasn't going to support me and what I really wanted to do.

I was scared to leave my two-income household, especially since I was still riding the roller coaster of cash flow, but I knew my heart couldn't afford to no longer have love. I had a hole in my heart where I wanted a loving relationship.

Luckily, along my life's journey I developed a lot of confidence and faith in myself. My mom and dad were always supportive and had always told me I could do anything and be anything I wanted. I don't remember them ever having money issues or having a negative mindset. Settling for relationships that don't serve them is something a lot of entrepreneurs have challenges with. They're scared to jump out into the unknown, or they don't trust themselves enough to leap. I wasn't going to live that way. I was thirty-five years old; I had my whole life ahead of me, and I deserved love, affection, and 100 percent support.

I decided to leave the marriage so I could pursue my dreams and find someone who would truly love me. I ventured out into the online dating world around 2007, and boy, do I have stories to tell about that! I treated dating like a business, and when you're in business, you have to market your business to get clients. I looked at the online dating world as a numbers game and started focusing on it in a very organized and intentional way.

In January 2012, something changed in me, and I knew it was time to find my Mr. Right. I went on my quest to find my *keeper husband*. I hired a six-thousand-dollar matchmaking service. I went to three relationship workshops out of town that cost two thousand dollars each so I could hone my skills around being in a loving relationship. (I learned a LOT about myself at those!) I also was active on four online dating websites. I worked the system like crazy. Probably 20 percent of my day every day was working on the dating aspect of my life. The other 80 percent of the time, I was working in my business. I find that most people don't put in this much effort to go after what they want, especially not in the dating world! They often don't even put in this much effort in their business, and then they wonder why they're not successful or don't make enough money.

On June 27, 2012, I had my first date with Jason Bittenbender. We met for sushi and continued on with an after-dinner drink because we didn't want to leave each other's side. Four hours later, we both knew this was it. He came with a bonus daughter, Riley, who was three-and-a-half years old. I was elated to find somebody with whom I could build a family without getting pregnant because that wasn't on the agenda for me.

Four months later, Jason moved into my house with Riley. Eleven years later, and we're living in a beautiful house with a loving dog, Luna, and life couldn't be better. It wasn't without challenges to get where we are today. In fact, when Jason proposed in 2014, we had planned to get married that year, but three weeks later, he was diagnosed with throat cancer. I said, "Oh no! You can't leave me yet—I just found you!"

He spent a year in treatments and had five surgeries, with me nursing him back to health. Luckily, he has been clear of cancer ever since, but it was a hard year. On top of that, in 2013, I had two total hip replacement surgeries that he had to help me with. These "life situations" taught me how important it was to be prepared for the "what if." I wouldn't have been able to spend half of my day every day for eight weeks straight taking care of Jason and his appointments if I didn't have systems and automated marketing, team, and sales processes set up in my business ahead of time. I didn't lose any income while I was taking care of him.

Entrepreneurs often wait until chaos hits and then realize how much they need their business to be more automated and systematized. But by then, they're too busy or distracted to do anything about it. You never know when something's going to happen to you or a loved one. You also never know when you'll have to make a big life transition such as a divorce.

You have to stop and set this stuff up before you need to, whether you have a business or not. Heck, my dad died before updating his eighteen-year-old will, and I was in probate for eighteen months, with attorney fees of more than twenty-three thousand dollars!

You want to be able to focus on what really matters *when it really matters*. Life is too short to settle for crappy people, crappy jobs, or crappy situations.

You deserve to achieve your biggest, most bodacious dreams ever!

You deserve to make as much money as you can possibly imagine!

You deserve to be loved fully, 100 percent, without question!

I want you to live a life you love being surrounded by people you love and who love you, and I want you to be extremely fulfilled in your career or business, whichever you pursue. I want you to love yourself fully, have faith, and believe in yourself. It will all work out in the end!

Katrina Sawa is the CEO and Founder of JumpstartYourBizNow.com and JumpstartPublishing.net. Since 2002, she has been lovingly known as The Jumpstart Your Biz Coach because she kicks her clients into high gear so they make more money doing what they love—and fast. She also makes sure they focus on the LOVE side of their life so they can enjoy a life full of both love and money.

Katrina is the creator of the Jumpstart Your Marketing & Sales System, international bestselling author with twenty books, including, *Love Yourself Successful, Jumpstart Your New Business Now* and the *Jumpstart Your _____(blank)* compilation book series. Katrina has a no-nonsense approach for showing entrepreneurs how to develop consistently profitable businesses by implementing proven marketing and business strategies.

As CEO of Jumpstart Publishing, Katrina helps entrepreneurs publish books that generate more clients and revenue with clear intention, purpose, and impactful marketing strategy.

Katrina has been featured on the Oprah and Friends XM Radio Network, ABC, The CW, and the *LA Tribune* in addition to dozens of print and online magazines and hundreds of podcasts. Katrina speaks to groups of all sizes, holds live training events, and masterminds virtually and in person. She lives in Northern California with her husband, Jason, and stepdaughter Riley.

To learn how to start, grow, and monetize your business to its fullest potential, access any of Katrina's free training videos, downloads, or one-on-one consults online on her website.

www.JumpstartYourBizNow.com

OVERCOME ADVERSITY: RISE ABOVE YOUR CIRCUMSTANCE

Liz Smith

I will never forget Friday, October 21. I was fourteen years old and had just started attending a new high school when I was told to go to the principal's office. I walked into the office and the principal greeted me with a solemn look on her face.

"Elizabeth, you need to go home; your dad will be sending a car for you," she said.

My heart started pounding. I thought, *Was I in trouble? What did I do? Why was I being sent home?* I immediately started crying.

When I got home, I saw my four younger brothers and my dad standing together. They weren't saying a word; you could have heard a pin drop. My dad looked at me with tears in his green eyes and said, "Beth, your mom just died."

I immediately responded, "What? I don't believe it!" My mom was such a loving person, such a breath of fresh air—why would God take her away? She was only forty-seven years old! I felt so vulnerable—and so angry at God.

That year, I had a difficult time adjusting at school. I lost my focus in the classroom, and I ended up failing that grade. I was devasted! Jamaican middle-class children are expected to excel, and my dad took that on as his responsibility. Although loving and caring, he also was very much of a disciplinarian. When I handed my dad my term report, I was terrified as I watched him slowly open the envelope. He glanced at the report, and then looked at me and said, "Elizabeth."

I thought, *Oh-oh, I'm in trouble! He's calling me Elizabeth, not Beth.*

After a long pause, he said, "I know you're still trying to get over the death of your mother. I am not mad at you, just disappointed. I know you will make it!"

Wow, that was a surprise from the disciplinarian! He then said, "Remember what your mother used to always say? 'I can do all things through Christ who strengthens me.'" We even had a plaque with that Bible verse from Philippians 4:13 displayed in our home.

As the years went by, that verse gradually became my lifeline. At the completion of high school, I was the recipient of a scholarship to study nursing in Ontario, Canada. Believing in a higher power gave me the strength and perseverance to step out of my comfort zone and travel to Canada from Jamaica. Moving to Canada wasn't just a culture shock—it was shockingly cold! I had to adjust to twenty degrees below zero! I dreaded it.

To add insult to injury, the nursing college modified their three-year program to an accelerated two-year program. During this time, there was a shortage of registered nurses in Canada, and this was a mandate from the Canadian government. To finish such a program in two years was very tough. I had to manage my time effectively and keep my grades up. I couldn't afford to fail—I was on a scholarship. Although overwhelmed at times, with perseverance I completed my studies, passed the Board of Registered Nurses exam, and got my license to practice nursing, which was also my green light to return to Jamaica.

However, within eighteen months of being home, I became disillusioned. The Jamaican government had not lived up to their commitment in the scholarship contract, and I was disappointed. Confused, I thought, *Should I stay or should I go?* I prayed about it, and the following week I got a letter from Terry, my best friend in nursing college, who had relocated to California. To my amazement, she wrote, "There is a shortage of RNs in California—come!"

This was divine intervention, an answer to prayer, and a confirmation from God. I took a leap of faith and boarded a nonstop flight to California and never looked back. I landed a job in a private hospital as an ER nurse, and within a year I was promoted to charge nurse. I kept focused, did the work, persevered through many challenges, and within two years I was promoted to nursing director of the evening shift with administrative responsibilities.

I knew I needed more formal education, so I earned a bachelor of science degree in business and started focusing on the "bigger picture." A position opened up for an assistant administrator, and without hesitation, I applied for the job and was delighted that I was the chosen candidate. I then pursued an advanced degree in business and earned my MBA from Pepperdine University.

Still missing my family and friends in Jamaica, I took a vacation to visit them. Upon returning to my office, the president of the hospital wanted to meet with me. His first comments were, "Welcome back Liz; now I know who has been doing the work around here." He mentioned that my boss was no longer there, and he wanted me to move into the vice president's office, a large, nicely furnished corner office with a window. My limited beliefs and doubts were challenged, and it felt like I was being put through the test in claiming my passion and purpose in life to be a leader. Within three months, though, I was promoted to vice president of Professional Services. With much required of me, I now had to learn how to effectively delegate and empower others.

Several years later, the hospital was sold and a new president was at the helm. About six months after this change, upon returning from my annual vacation, the new President wanted to meet with me. I thought, *The last time I returned and the president met with me, I got a promotion—I wonder what it will be this time.* Well, this time the tables were turned; instead of a promotion, I was laid off along with several other executives. I was devasted; I had dedicated twenty-four years of my life to the hospital, ten years in my current executive position. I was the first woman in that position, and I had held that position the longest in the history of the hospital. Initially I was angry; however, as an advocate for women in leadership, I was determined not to be discouraged.

Stepping out of my comfort zone, I interviewed for and accepted an executive position in public health with a well-established medical center in Los Angeles. At that time, there was a need for a culture shift in my department, and this gave me the opportunity to engage the staff for their "buy-in" while mentoring and coaching them.

I recall a particular incident with one of my managers when coaching was very instrumental. She needed to take a more critical and strategic approach in aligning some of the community programs with the vision and mission of the Medical Center. This initially was an uphill battle for her as she had split her loyalty between her employer and a well-established philanthropic group that contributes to financially sustaining many of the community programs. Our meeting could have been very confrontational; however, after a few coaching sessions, she was able to gain clarity and embrace the "bigger picture." By confronting the limited beliefs and self-doubts that were stopping her, she implemented the necessary changes to transform her department, and she elevated the caliber and effectiveness of the community programs offered. To that end, the medical center was the recipient of a National Award for Community Service.

Over the years, the healthcare industry experienced many changes. The medical center was not exempt and became fiscally challenged. This resulted in several positions being eliminated, including mine. In life, it seems that the only thing constant is change, and once again, I was challenged to respond to my new circumstances.

As I reflect on my life, I recognize that the many challenges I went through were actually stepping stones toward preparing myself to contribute to the lives of many women in diverse industries who are up to the leadership challenges. It was Mahatma Gandhi who said, "Be the change you want to see." I asked myself, "Why not now? If not now, when?" I am passionate about leadership and the purpose of engaging other ladies committed to fulfilling their destiny.

Ladies, we need to be at the table—our voices need to be heard. We have a significant contribution to make to the world. At times, we are our worst enemy when we let our limited beliefs and self-doubt get in the way, eroding our self-confidence. The time has come to rise above our circumstances! Remember, you were created on purpose, with a purpose, and for a purpose. Believe in yourself, step out in faith, overcome the obstacles getting in your way, and be the great human being you were created to be.

Liz Smith is an executive coach and keynote speaker. As president and founder of Peak Performance Leadership Journey, she coaches professional women who aspire to great achievements to overcome their limited beliefs and self-doubts so they can elevate their self-confidence, live life passionately, and fulfill their destiny with enormous impact. Liz holds an MBA from Pepperdine University and an executive master of leadership degree from the University of Southern California.

Liz has spent most of her professional life in the healthcare industry, where she has held several leadership positions. In addition, she has been actively involved in various organization boards where she has been instrumental in implementing change and contributing to success. During her career as an executive in healthcare, she experienced numerous changes and navigated through much uncertainty in a very complex industry.

With more than twenty-five years of leadership experience, Liz is passionate about encouraging women to rise above their self-imposed limits, take on the difficult assignments, advance their career, have a voice, and assume top leadership positions. The time has come for more women to meet leadership challenges; have a seat at the table; lead with integrity, values, and purpose; and make a significant difference. Liz takes a personal interest in fostering learning environments as a platform to challenge emerging and current leaders to excel in their leadership skills, knowledge, and abilities while embracing the inevitable changes in the twenty-first century.

www.PeakPerformanceLeadershipJourney.com

SURFING THROUGH CHAOS: HOW TO PADDLE BACK TO JOY AND PURPOSE

Bonnie Stevens

Sitting on a surfboard, gazing at the lush southern flanks of Haleakala Crater, watching wispy clouds drift lazily across the island and feeling the unusually calm, refreshingly cool Pacific Ocean lap against my legs in the warm sunshine, I was miserable. *Can you really lose your joy*, I wondered?

How I got here, emotionally and physically, can be explained by the chaos happening all around me, causing a cosmic shift in the universe. My universe.

The early tremors of change began when my husband and I sold our Northern Arizona mountain home quickly. Too quickly. We had no solid plan for what would happen next. This led to us living one hundred miles apart. My youngest son became my roommate in an impossibly crowded one-bedroom condo.

The seismic shifting grew stronger as my mom, oldest sister, and oldest brother all became fatally ill. My life had become an endless cycle of driving from the mountains to the desert to help my family, all while working too many jobs. I was exhausted and overwhelmed.

THE LOSS OF JOY

Arizona sunsets are known worldwide. The vibrant neon oranges, hot pinks, and magentas are stunning. Every sunset is a mesmerizing new painting. But suddenly, I had no interest in sunsets. I'd look away. I just didn't care about them. I also didn't care about music, food, fashion, or fun. Who was this girl?

The thing about falling deep into despair is that there is supposed to be a hero to step in and save you, right? Where was my hero?

I decided that *someone* should pose an intervention. *That's what* I *would do*, I thought self-righteously, *if someone I loved were getting beaten down by life. I would pluck them right out of that situation and put them in a safe, comfortable, beautiful place where they could relax, think without distraction, and regain their optimism and strength. I'd feed them healthy delicious meals, bring in animals to provide comfort, enroll them in a yoga class, remind them of their greatness, and insist they take a week off, far away from that thing that was stressing them out.* So where were *my* intervenors?

During a news interview a few years ago, actress Cybill Shepherd told me, "We all need mothering sometimes." This felt like one of those times, except my mom was fighting her own battle of lost memories.

I got very still and asked for guidance. Oddly, my inner voice said, "Go surf."

My Christian friends were pretty sure I misunderstood the message, which must have been, "Go serve." Nonetheless, I began exploring surf camps on the internet.

I found Swell Women in Hawaii. But spending five thousand dollars seemed hugely irresponsible. And where would the money come from?

And that's when my mom reached out to me through the fog of dementia. She granted each of her children five thousand dollars. Within two weeks, I was on my way to my own intervention, to the healing place of Maui, under the care and guidance of my new surfer friends.

THIRD EYE BLIND

Upon arriving at Kahului Airport, a big white van picked me up. I didn't know where I was going, but it didn't matter. I figured I was already lost, so a big white van inviting me out of the afternoon trade winds and toward the beach seemed like the right direction.

The hotel was everything you'd expect on a tropical island: swaying palm trees, soft sand, crashing waves, and tan men in Hawaiian shirts handing out pineapple rum drinks. Somewhere inside of me, a little surfer girl was pounding her fists, demanding to come out and play.

I explored the view from my second-floor balcony. There was a ton of commotion going on down below. Upon investigation, I learned that the rock band, Third Eye Blind, was setting up for a concert on the grass, RIGHT UNDER MY BALCONY! The irony of the rock band's name and my current state of mind were lost on me. I couldn't see how the universe was pushing me toward change. Regardless, I was definitely going to this concert.

By early evening, I had made friends with the security guard at the entrance. Turns out he was from Arizona! We had a lot to talk about, and my new friend walked me right through the gate and straight up to the front of the crowd. I danced like no one was watching, rocked out with the band members who were within a few feet of me, and still wasn't paying attention to yet another sign as Third Eye Blind played "Semi-Charmed Life."

COULD JOY BE SURFACING?

It had been three days. I adored my new tribe, and I loved the schedule and the fact that I had no responsibilities except to show up. I devoured the locally grown flavors, admired the yoga and surf instructors, and couldn't think of anyplace I would rather be.

I was having a wonderful time. But no matter how hard I tried, I couldn't hang on to the good feelings. So, on that August morning, sitting on a surfboard, gazing at the lush southern flanks of Haleakala Crater, I couldn't understand why I was numb.

As I sat there, absorbed in grief, I sensed movement. I slowly turned my head to the right as a big, dark shadow was surfacing, ever so slowly. There was no one close by, and no waves in sight. I wasn't going anywhere. All I could do was watch with great anticipation to learn what was in the sea next to me.

When the thing in the water popped its head out with a huge gasp, all I could do was gasp as well—and then smile, a big, genuine, toothy smile. "Hello, Turtle," I said softly.

He wasn't in a hurry, and I didn't have anywhere to go. So, there we were, hanging out in the Pacific Ocean, me and a granddaddy of a sea turtle. Together, we turned our gaze back to the island, taking in the beauty of Haleakala and the serenity of the moment.

A feeling of lightness came over me. I've heard that dolphins saved lost sailors by leading them back to land. Did this gentle creature come to save me?

In that instant, I saw Maui in all her brilliance—vibrant colors, the grace of the landscape, palm trees swaying. As the turtle had found its way to the surface, so had my joy. My perception had shifted. I felt at peace. Grounded. Grateful.

Later, I googled the spiritual meaning of the sea turtle. It carries the world on its back yet is grounded under the weight. Sea turtles symbolize peace and emotional strength.

THE GARDEN OF EDEN

I once asked Apollo 12 astronaut Alan Bean what went through his mind as he was standing on the moon surrounded by gray and looking back at Earth.

"I realized we live in the Garden of Eden," he said.

The Garden of Eden, I thought, *a place of beauty and abundance—everything we need.*

After returning to the mainland, I had renewed strength and energy, along with great enthusiasm for life and a calm acceptance of the chaos around me. Perhaps it was the Aloha Spirit, the healing powers of Maui, or the Garden of Eden revealed. Whatever it was, I will never forget my journey back to joy, the decision I made to go out and find it, and the positive, intentional steps I took to regain my optimism, inner strength, and purpose.

I was relearning how to thoroughly absorb the big moments, appreciate the little ones, and share time patiently with those who would be leaving their bodies soon. I was distancing my heart from people and habits that were causing me pain, and I would soon be meeting the love of my life.

It's easy to lose ourselves when change sends shock waves through our lives. We might forget our value, dim our light, and ask for less. Today, I won't settle for a semi-charmed life, and I hope you won't either. That's why I illuminate women who are hungry for their best life by showing them how to shine brighter and embrace their unique story so they can step into the spotlight, increase their visibility and inspire others to share their gifts.

Bonnie Stevens is an Emmy award-winning documentary producer, international speaker, journalist, author, editor, public relations consultant, and former television news anchor. Her work has appeared on CNN, PBS, major network-affiliated stations, and NPR's Northern Arizona affiliate. Her reporting has taken her trekking across Panama's forests, snorkeling over Hawaii's coral reefs, climbing to remote Grand Canyon springs, and exploring moon like terrain with astronauts and scientists.

As comfortable on a ski slope as she is in the boardroom, Bonnie is a lifelong student of nature, science, and business. She has worked with Babbitt Ranches, W. L. Gore & Associates, the Forest Service, Arizona Snowbowl, and Northern Arizona University and is the editor of *Flagstaff Business News* and *Quad Cities Business News*.

In addition, for thirty years she was instrumental in developing and implementing the Flagstaff Festival of Science. Bonnie has been recognized for her work in journalism, forestry, science, and leadership, is an ATHENA Award recipient, and promotes women leadership through the Quad Cities ATHENA Awards. Passionate about education, Bonnie, together with her mentor, pioneering news anchor Mary Jo West, founded the Mary Jo West Excellence in Communication Scholarship.

Bonnie is married to Rich Naden, mom to Logan Holmes, Tyler and his wife, Ashley, stepmom to Shayne and Chad Plesa-Naden and nana to Makenzie, Jackson, and Quinn. An Arizonan since age two, she offers inspiration and information through her vodcast, *Zonie Living: Business, Adventure and Leadership*, and her book *Life Lessons from a Zonie Girl: How to Stay Sunny, Grounded and Resilient.*

www.BonnieStevensArizona.com

SHE NEEDS HOPE

Bethany Sunny

Shock . . . confusion . . . frustration! What do you mean the degree I flew three thousand miles for and paid thousands of dollars to get "is no longer being offered"?

Let me start from the beginning.

My love for teaching was obvious even as a small child. Instead of playing with dolls, making mud pies, or dressing up, I would invite my friends over to "play" school: They would sit down and listen as I would teach. I have no idea what I "taught" them, but they must have liked it because they kept coming back.

As I got older, I found every opportunity to teach and impact young people's lives—Sunday School teacher, summer intern, camp counselor—I loved working with teenagers who were going through such a difficult yet pivotal time in their lives. The skills God has given me all revolved around teaching: taking the complex and making it simple, listening and hearing more than the words people say, and having a sincere passion for people. So, picking a career was easy for me: I wanted to be a youth director in a church.

Growing up with my father as the pastor of what we would call a "mega church" these days, I was always at church. During my teen years, Dad preached three morning services and one evening service on Sundays and a midweek service on Wednesdays. My mom was excellent at holding everything together. She loved being a pastor's wife and was devoted to God and her family. Her passion was children's ministry, earning a BA from Bob Jones University and later becoming children's director at the church.

When it came to a college degree for me, I really hoped there was a degree in youth ministry. As I looked at multiple schools, I hadn't found one—until one day, a family friend's son visited us from Arizona. He had just graduated from Liberty Baptist University with a degree in youth ministries! I was so excited. I researched the school and the degree and quickly applied. I was beyond thrilled when my acceptance letter arrived.

In August, with many mixed emotions, I boarded a plane in Los Angeles to attend a college I had never seen, located in Virginia. I was on my own and off to a new adventure.

Before I knew it, I was in Virginia, staring at a small dorm room I would share with three other girls. My roommates hadn't arrived yet, and suddenly it hit me. I was alone, knowing no one, at a large university. My excitement had worn off, and reality hit hard. What had I done?

Lost in my thoughts, feeling homesick, and fighting back tears, my first roommate arrived with her parents. They introduced themselves and began getting their daughter settled in. As we started talking, they realized I was alone and invited me to go to dinner with them. I quickly accepted and have been forever thankful for their generosity. It made my first day on campus much easier.

Soon the campus began to fill with students, and registration day came quickly. I was eager to select my classes and get started immersing myself in college life. It wasn't my first year in college or my first dorm experience, but it was the first time being so far away from home. As I entered the large room crawling with students, I found my bearings and began the registration process. I received the book outlining the available degrees and required classes. Looking at the list, I didn't see the youth ministries degree. I found the right person and asked where to find the classes for the youth ministries degree. Her answer: They were no longer offering it.

WHAT?

"What do you mean the degree is no longer being offered?" I was in shock. Now what would I do?

I registered for general education classes, a Bible class, and the recommended one class available for women who wanted the youth ministries degree. I decided I didn't need to make any major decisions as I had required classes to take. I made friends, continued at Liberty Baptist University, and plugged into the local church, where I had many opportunities to work with students in the youth department.

Even though the direction of my career had changed, my love for working with and impacting people for Christ never changed. But as they say, "Life happens." Instead of allowing God to direct my path, I decided to make my own. The path I took was not bad in and of itself, but I knew it wasn't the path God wanted me to travel. I took a job in corporate America with the plan of "moving up the proverbial corporate ladder." I enjoyed promotions, flying to new places for business, and meeting my future husband.

Then everything changed again. The economy was on a downturn, and layoffs were sweeping through the company. Although my boss had prepared me for the probability of being laid off, when the day came, I felt angry, depressed, and even shocked. These emotions surprised me, since I had been warned about the layoffs ahead of time. This experience helped me understand the deep feelings attached to being let go from a company you were fully invested in.

God knew where He wanted me to go, even if I didn't. My experience opened a door for me to begin teaching. It was early 1990s, and computers were appearing on employees' desks. I began freelancing as a computer trainer for companies such as Nestle, JPL, and Disney, and this allowed me to start my first business, Software Training Resources. I was on a new adventure and loved it.

However, after owning several businesses, my desire to impact people through the Bible increased. In 2018, this passion, along with seeing so many young people turning away from God, began to form into the idea of creating an online ministry—a ministry that would focus on providing resources, Bible studies, and biblical resources for women.

In my head, it sounded so easy. I had the technical skills as I had been building websites since the early 1990s, I had many resources available to me through my dad's ministry, and I loved teaching. What could go wrong?

Everything . . .

There were so many ways I could create the ministry, but every time I began planning, I would get stuck. Then doubts and a lack of self-confidence would grow inside me. As I researched what was already out there, I began feeling less and less capable, and I became depressed over my inability to do what God wanted me to do. I let self-doubt and insecurities overtake me, and the days of deciding how to create the ministry turned into years.

Then out of the blue, my world was rocked again . . .

In 2019, my mom unexpectedly passed away, and I moved in with my dad to take care of him. In early 2020, COVID-19 invaded the world, and then in late 2020, my brother and his family decided to move out of California, and my brother asked me if my family, including my dad, wanted to move with them. I had always been open to moving out of California, but their timetable was aggressive. Through prayer and much discussion, we collectively decided to move to Tennessee. We made the decision in January 2021, and by May, we were completely relocated. As you can imagine, those few months were a whirlwind of planning, packing, selling and buying homes, and establishing a new life in a city where I knew no one.

One of the many benefits of this move is that God provided me with two wonderful godly women who quickly became amazing friends. God always provides what we need when we need it. It is our responsibility to follow Him and allow Him to work in and through our lives. I was finally ready.

Although I have had many wonderful friends helping me along the way, God has used these women to get me to where I am today. They provided insight, encouragement, and godly advice that has helped me to bring my passion into reality. Finally my online ministry, She Needs Hope, was born.

The road has been long and bumpy, but I know I am where God has called me, and I am eager to share my new ministry, which is designed to bring hope found in God's Word. Using my skills as a teacher and my ability to make the complex simple, I teach and encourage women who are looking for answers, hope, and resources for themselves and their families through studying the Bible. I invite you to join me in this adventure! No matter where you are in life—whether you are new to Jesus, doubting God's Word, or longing for a deeper walk with God, this is the place for you. I look forward to seeing you there!

Meet **Bethany Sunny**, a successful business owner, published author, and the visionary founder behind She Needs Hope. This online ministry is designed to help those who are doubting their faith, confused when reading the Bible, or wanting to dig deeper into God's Word.

Growing up in a loving, Bible-believing family as the daughter of a pastor, Bethany possesses an unshakable foundation built upon God's Word. But her personal choices did not always reflect this strong faith. In 1990, feeling disillusioned by unmet expectations, she embarked on a path separate from God's will.

Though her story is not a "jaw-dropping" one, her decision to rededicate her life to Christ led her on a journey of asking hard questions, finding good resources, and seeking answers through studying the Bible.

Bethany is now on a mission to help other women on their faith journey. With thirty years of business experience and using her God-given teaching skills, she launched She Needs Hope in

2023, providing biblical resources and a loving community where women can find encouragement and accountability.

www.SheNeedsHope.com

PROPEL YOUR HEALTH FORWARD

Bonnie Taub

Imagine this scenario: In 1957 when I was in sixth grade, a classmate raised her hand and asked to go to the bathroom. As she was walking toward the front of the room, she keeled over and fell on the floor with a thud. Everyone stopped what they were doing as the teacher rushed over. Time stood still, and the next thing I knew she was being carried out of the classroom by the school nurse. I have no idea how the nurse got there or how the girl was revived. Somehow the teacher got everyone's attention and class resumed. But I couldn't focus. I had never seen anyone faint before, and I couldn't get the image out of my mind. I'll never forget this student's name (Doris) or what she looked like (small, very thin, dark short hair).

A while later, the school nurse came in to tell us what happened. You see, Doris only had a cup of coffee for breakfast. Apparently, that had been her daily breakfast for several years. The nurse then proceeded to give us a lesson on breakfast being the most important meal of the day. She said it gave us energy and provided nutrients that made us healthy and strong. It allowed us to be productive and able to focus on our schoolwork. She also stressed that breakfast should be a hot cooked meal. I really wasn't sure what that all meant, but it made quite an impression on me.

You see, my mother wasn't interested in cooking or cleaning. We had a cleaning girl that came in every week. Our meals came in boxes or cans. Everything was prepackaged. My sister and I ate cold cereal or pop-tarts for breakfast, which I could easily set out, as I was the oldest. My mother loved to spend her time doing crossword puzzles, reading books, or playing mah-jongg. She was very smart and had graduated college at age nineteen with a degree in foreign languages. My dad, on the other hand, never went to college, but instead got his education in the Army and ran his own business after World War II. He worked very hard and kept long hours, so he was never home for dinner. He missed our graduations and other special events; there were lots of missed promises. (Although I do have a fond memory of going with my dad to the last game at Dodger Stadium before the team moved to Los Angeles. I also remember going with him to the movies to see westerns on the weekends).

At ten years old, I was a very shy, introverted girl. I never spoke up in school, and I panicked if a teacher asked me a question. I never initiated making plans with friends; instead I always waited for them to call me. But now, I was faced with a dilemma: What to do about this breakfast situation? Should I confront my mother or just start making breakfast myself?

That day when I got home from school, I asked my mother, "Why don't you get up in the morning and fix breakfast for us before we go to school?" She just looked at me in astonishment as if to say, "Am I supposed to do that?" Needless to say, I realized that if I wanted things to change, I would have to do it myself. So, every day until I went off to college, I got up early and cooked breakfast. Eventually there were three more children, making a total of five. Usually, I made bacon and scrambled eggs. To this day, that is still my favorite breakfast, only now I cook turkey bacon with organic free-range eggs, and I use a dairy-free cheese alternative.

Thus began my journey with food.

Fast-forward: After college, I married the love of my life. This was before women's lib. The norm was that women got married and had children. Being the oldest of five, I figured I already had my family. After staying home for several years, I grew tired of having to ask my husband for money whenever I wanted something, so I entered the workforce. And guess what? I got a job in a bagel shop, working with food!

At the bagel shop, I worked behind the scenes. I learned how to cook the bagels in the oven and put on all the different toppings, and I got pretty good at it. I made all the different varieties from cream cheese to sliced lox, and I also made a variety of salads and learned how to make catering platters. When the store was sold, the new owner fired everyone. So I got a job next door at Carvel! Again food—the universe was giving me signs. Here I learned how to decorate ice-cream cakes and run soft-serve ice-cream machines.

Around this time, my marriage hit a rough patch. My husband "thought" he found a new love and decided to leave. I now needed to find a career to be able to support myself if my marriage didn't work out. I had been getting regular massages which was keeping me healthy, both physically and mentally. I decided I wanted to be able to do this for others, so I went to massage school. There I got the training I needed, and I learned how nutrition affects the physical body. As it turned out, I was quite good at massage, and I got a job on staff teaching both theory and technique courses. I even worked in the student clinic, supervising the students in their clinical rounds. I now have my own practice, specializing in lymph drainage therapy.

My journey into health continued as a result of my husband's health crisis. (Yes, I am still married to the same man who left me.) After he retired from teaching, he became quite ill with Crohn's disease, an inflammatory bowel disease of the small intestine. Until he was properly diagnosed, he was wasting away and almost died. Once again, I was thrust into a situation where food and nutrition were of paramount importance. Western medicine focuses on treating illness and disease with drugs and often misses the food connection. Don't get me wrong, drugs can be life-saving and definitely have their place. If it weren't for them, my husband would have died. But knowing how the body works and getting to the root cause is just as important. Even though my husband now is in remission, if he is exposed to certain foods, his symptoms come back. That's how important nutrition is.

While he was in the hospital for several months, working with a Crohn's specialist to find the right medication, I went back to school to learn about nutrition and how it affects the body's overall health. At the time, he was having about twenty bowel movements a day and trying to stop losing weight. His friends didn't think he was going to make it. What helped quite a bit was his mindset. He was determined not to have his illness take a toll on me, his caregiver. You see, I had to put my life on hold for several years. I couldn't travel and go to conferences and conventions. I had to stop being a teaching assistant at The Chickly Health Institute in the lymph drainage program. I loved doing all these things; they fill my soul, and it was hard to give them up.

Thankfully, by changing his diet along with taking medication, he is no longer tied to the house. We are able to go out to dinner and not have to worry about running home. We are able to travel again and live a more normal life. Three years ago, we were able to travel to Florida from Arizona for my niece's wedding. Through my own journey in making dietary changes, I have eliminated nasal congestion, gas and bloating, dark circles under my eyes, body inflammation, and excess weight. I sleep better and enjoy life. I did this through my own studies and lots of hard work. It would have been easier if I had had a nutritional counselor guiding me.

We are all individuals, and what is right for one person may not be right for someone else. If you are struggling with your digestive health, I would love to assist you on your journey so you can be empowered to make the changes you need.

Bonnie Taub is a licensed massage therapist who specializes in lymph drainage therapy. She earned her A.O.S degree in 1998 at

The New York College of Health Professions and her B.P.S at the same school in 1999. In 1967, Bonnie graduated with a B.S. in mathematics with a minor in education from S.U.N.Y at Stony Brook. She earned a certificate as a holistic health counselor from The Institute for Integrative Nutrition in 2004. Bonnie went on to study at The Nutritional Therapy Association, graduating as a functional nutritional therapy practitioner in 2017. In May 2022, Bonnie graduated from Restorative Wellness Solutions as a master restorative wellness practitioner.

Bonnie established Your Harmonized Health, a combination massage therapy and functional nutritional practice, in 2018 after moving from New York to Arizona. While in New York, her massage therapy practice flourished. In Scottsdale, Arizona, she is able to incorporate G.I. MAP and MRT testing in her RWP program. A hands-on functional evaluation, learned at NTA, ensures the individualization of the program. These tools empower Bonnie's clients to make unique choices that are right for them.

www.YourHarmonizedHealth.com

ON THE OTHER SIDE OF YOUR TERROR BARRIER

Olivia Vo

My knuckles turned white as I clutched the American Express credit card in my hand. I could feel my whole body grimace, and the knots in my stomach grew tighter and tighter. My heart pulsed in rhythm to all the thoughts pummeling through my mind:

Am I ready for this?
Is it the responsible thing to do?
What about my husband?
Is it safe?
Do I have the money?

My breath came out in short, rapid bursts. This was it. While staring at the payment and registration page before me, I had come face-to-face with my personal terror barrier.

This wall loomed large, and I desperately wanted to scale it and go over the top. I knew that I owed it to myself to see what was on the other side.

The music faded out of the Zoom room, and Arvee Robinson's voice boomed out loudly, interrupting my looping thoughts, "Signups are coming in fast! We have one spot left open for the Speaking Mastermind Retreat in Puerto Vallarta, Mexico! Who is it going to be?"

Despite the tingling sensation electrifying my body, I declared out loud, "It's me! It's going to be me! I am signing up right now!"

My clammy, sticky fingers pounded on the keyboard as I entered my credit card information and hit submit.

The questions still lingered in my mind, and my inner judge made sure I was accountable in answering each one:

- *Yes, I am ready and this is something that have been wanting for a very long time to go on a retreat.*
- *I am acting responsibly in moving forward with a new skill and speaking career.*
- *My husband is supportive of me and would not stand in the way of my personal growth.*
- *I trust Arvee who has made many visits to Puerto Vallarta to vet the area. I will be traveling with a group.*
- *There is money on this credit card, and I will find a way to pay it back.*

As I mentally gave each response, the knots in my stomach became looser and looser, and finally I was breathing again at a calm, measured pace.

"Congratulations, Olivia! You are in!" And suddenly my picture appeared in the spotlight along with the other retreat participants and hearty applause lifted me up. Instead of having to climb the terror barrier, I levitated over it.

"And by the way, Olivia, I'd love for you to do some laughter yoga with us during the retreat."

My heart swelled even further with joy. This was what I needed to hear as confirmation. On the other side of the terror barrier lay the zone of opportunity. Not only was I going on this retreat to craft my signature talk with Arvee's technique and formula, but I also received a wonderful invitation to share and express my favorite laughter yoga exercises.

Yet, once I arrived in Mexico, there were still more terror barriers to overcome. This time, unresolved feelings that I had with my previous career in recruiting and staffing started to surface. In my first year of entrepreneurship, I dove headfirst into digital upskilling and learning about social media marketing and livestreaming. I also wanted to get as far away as possible from recruiting to do something creative, so I pursued training in Laughter Yoga. Going through laughter training and receiving my certification as an instructor helped me tremendously in reclaiming some of the joy I'd lost in my job. I got involved with many online collaborations for virtual events and book anthologies. It seemed natural to me that I would segue into speaking. But would I be taken seriously if I chose to focus on speaking about laughter as my topic?

I am so grateful for having the retreat environment in which I could confront my terror barrier. Perhaps being in a new setting surrounded by a supportive loving community of other women and the personal sincere coaching from Arvee allowed me to process the forgotten feelings that I had been running away from when I made the decision to leave my job. I realized that if I wanted to be the gal with the heart-shaped glasses and speak about laughter as well as demo and guide people in activating their own laughter, it was time for me to truly embrace and "own it."

With Arvee's training, I successfully developed and delivered my signature talk on "The Power of Laughter and How It Can Help You to Be More Creative." I received tremendous positive feedback, and I felt in harmony with my natural essence, thoughts, and feelings in this divine moment of self-reinvention. My personal story, spirit, and style were finally coming together. What got me over the terror barrier were the many hands of my colleagues that graciously extended down to me and pulled me up. Once over the terror barrier, there is much freedom in the realm of possibility.

Prior to me taking the stage to speak, Arvee gave me the most amazing gift of all: a purple heart-shaped rock that had the word *poweful* engraved on it. At first glance, I was disappointed to see the typo—the "r" was missing! As I examined it closer, though, I burst into laughter. I became a powerful, charismatic speaker that day; I incorporated the lesson into my talk and shared that the "r" stood for a **r**eminder that we don't have to strive for perfection all the time; there is also a certain beauty in imperfect things and people. "R" also stood for **r**emember to laugh by choice and not leave it up to chance. I cherish this heart-shaped stone and lesson very much, and I always carry it with me.

Since speaking at Casa de Influencia and becoming an international keynote speaker, my signature talk is now "The Healing Power of Laughter and How It Can Help You to Forgive." I've further expanded my laughter exercises to include an adaptation of the four phrases of the Hawaiian prayer of *Ho'oponopono* ("I'm sorry; Please forgive me; Thank you; I love you"). Each time I deliver my laughter meditation to various groups, I heal the wound of past hurts and most importantly, I've been able to honor my intuition, which has led me on my current path of self-discovery and purpose.

I wear my heart-shaped glasses to radiate out love and joy and make other people smile and feel at ease in my presence. I want to win others over and positively affect their mood and happiness. The same empathy and compassion I so readily give to others, I can also extend to my inner judge and practice my own self-compassion by seeing myself with loving eyes.

WHAT DOES THE TERROR BARRIER LOOK LIKE FOR YOU?

According to the late Bob Proctor, the terror barrier is made up of the subconscious limiting beliefs and fears that prevent us from achieving our goals and living our best lives. These limiting beliefs and fears can be so powerful and overwhelming that they create a psychological barrier to hold us back from taking action and pursuing our dreams.

The terror barrier is a manifestation of our deep-seated fears, such as fear of failure, fear of rejection, fear of the unknown, and fear of success. We can have both emotional and physiological responses, such as intense feelings of anxiety and doubt and increased heart rate, rapid breathing, sweating, and muscle tension.

There may be crucial moments when you are facing your own terror barrier in starting a business, overcoming addictions, pursuing creative passions, being a public speaker, or attempting athletic or physical challenges. When you recognize your symptoms, don't ignore them or look for a quick fix; rather lean into them and push past that initial fear.

You can overcome the terror barrier by challenging your limiting beliefs, by focusing on the present moment and the positive feeling that this is something you truly desire and have been waiting for, and by taking one micro action step at a time. When you feel your entire body tense up, learn to breathe and relax into each tense area one by one, and return the feeling to your hands and toes. Practice positive self-talk and visualize the new you who will have crossed over the terror barrier! You can repeat to yourself, "I am capable. I am confident. I am deserving." You can also seek the support of trusted mentors, coaches, leaders, and colleagues to help you with coping strategies.

Finally, hold space for self-compassion while you are in your terror barrier and cultivate a personal growth mindset that you can reinvent yourself at any given time. You are building new evidence against your limiting beliefs.

There are so many rewards waiting for you on the other side of your terror barrier as you move into the zone of opportunity and realm of possibility. You will find renewed self-confidence, personal transformation, satisfaction and fulfillment, and increased resilience. You may also be stepping into a new purpose in your life.

The next time that you are faced with your terror barrier, I want to encourage you to look in the mirror and recite this poem with feeling:

The terror barrier is quite scary,
It makes me feel very wary,
Tame the resistance,
Pursue with persistence,
I'll break through and be legendary.

Olivia Vo, The Savvy Social Strategist, is an international keynote speaker, professional emcee, international Amazon bestselling author, and joyful humorist. She has spoken on many virtual stages as well as in person at Casa de Influencia in Puerto Vallarta, Mexico; UNF's College of Education and Human Services in Jacksonville, Florida; and bLU Talks at Harvard Graduate School of Education in Cambridge, Massachusetts. She is instantly recognizable by her colorful heart-shaped glasses, and her enthusiasm and energy brighten the lives of those she meets.

A 2022 graduate of the USA Women Entrepreneurship Cooperative and the heart-centered founder of Savvy Social Pro Enterprises, Olivia specializes in online collaborations for LinkedIn social media training, book anthology projects, and live-stream events and promotions. Olivia likes to teach her S-A-V-V-Y approach when it comes to LinkedIn, helping clients to uncover their unique **S**kills, **A**ttributes, **V**alues, **V**ictories, and **Y**oung-at-Heart activities. This acronym has helped many to understand what to include in their profiles and content creation.

As a member of AATH (Association for Applied Therapeutic Humor), Olivia is currently enrolled in a three-year program with The Humor Academy to earn her Humor Professional Certification and has been trained in Laughter Yoga. She is available to speak on the health benefits of playful laughter exercises for your organization or event, and/or be considered as a meeting opener and closer to facilitate memorable and energizing experiences for your audiences.

www.LinkTr.ee/OliviaSavvyPro

PASSION AND PERSISTENCE

Dr. Joan E. Wakeland

What is it that fuels individuals to take actions to fulfill their dreams? How do they defy dream stealers? Is it the synergistic combination of passion and persistence? These are questions that I have asked myself. I was curious to know what I needed to learn to be successful.

I needed to learn to prioritize and stay focused. I needed to fulfill my commitments, over-delivering and under-promising! I needed to build strong relationships with influencers. It was important for me to ostracize the negative, energy leakers from my life. It was important to be able to recognize distractions.

The following contributing factors that have influenced me may also influence others:

- I desire a good lifestyle for myself and my child.
- I am committed to giving a fair day's work for a fair day's pay.
- I like recognition for doing a good job, and I enjoy my career because I was doing what I wanted to do. Therefore, I gave of my best.
- I live by the Golden Rule, treating people the way I want them to treat me.
- I have been blessed with a great network of friends, and I try to be a friend first.
- Relationships help increase my net worth!
- Connections can catapult you into areas you initially just dream of.

- Seizing the opportunity at the right time is important.
- I don't procrastinate—it is the thief of time and money!
- I don't respect people who tell me I CAN'T, and I do my best to prove them wrong!
- I've learned to listen and maintain eye contact with others.
- I stay in the present moment.

I have realized that it is not only passion—it is the combination of passion and persistence that allows individuals to take action. Taking action brings results—so follow your passion. Don't be afraid to go for it!

Passion and persistence both break barriers. These two words are the drivers of success. You actually become the person you believe you will become. Let's look at the lives of a few individuals who had a dream and who desired to change their circumstances.

Entertainers: Elvis Presley, Jerry Lee Lewis, Richard Valens, Johnny Cash, Ray Charles, Stevie Wonder, and Bob Marley all had a passion for music; they wanted to give of their best. Because they practiced regularly, they became confident when it was time for them to go onstage. That's when they were fired up! That's where emotions were expressed! That's where they were discovered as people liked their music. These entertainers all liked to perform and became successful because they were driven by their passion.

TV/ movies: Walt Disney was four million dollars in debt to the Bank of America back in 1944. Yet he persisted with his Mickey Mouse idea, and years later, Walt Disney theme parks entertain both young and old. His dream, his passion for animation, and his legacy live on years after his death.

Sidney Poitier KBE was a poor teenager from the Caribbean who came to America to start his life. He was laughed at for his

Caribbean accent and rejected for his poor reading skills, but Sidney Poitier took the rejection as a challenge. He knew he wanted to become an actor. He became unstoppable and achieved his goal. He was positive that the written word was the way to a better life; therefore, he read newspapers between his shifts as a dishwasher. For six months, he worked persistently to improve his reading. He struggled to learn and to understand what he read. He listened to the radio consistently. He practiced by repeating every word to modify his accent. He was passionate about achieving his dream!

He offered to serve as an unpaid janitor in exchange for taking classes at the theater's school because he didn't have the tuition. When you are hungry, when you want something bad enough, you will find a way. His teachers had little faith in him, but he persisted anyway. The preferred actor (Harry Belafonte) was unable to appear onstage one night, and Poitier was allowed to substitute for him. His performance was seen by a Broadway director who offered him a small role in an all-Black production. Poitier, who had failed to impress his teachers in the classroom, needed that chance to prove them wrong. His passion coupled with persistence catapulted him to a lifestyle he dreamed of. He became one of the best actors and refused to play certain roles if he thought the role was demeaning. He was the first Black actor to win the Academy Award for Best Actor in 1964. Sidney Poitier KBE was resilient, persistent, and passionate. He not only became the successful actor he envisioned—he also became a film director and a diplomat. He was even granted an honorary knighthood by Queen Elizabeth II for his contribution to the arts.

Steve Harvey was ridiculed by his classmates and his teacher. Steve had a big dream; his vision was to be on TV. His teacher did not have that vision for him so she shot his idea down. With the support from his father and prayers to the Almighty, he persisted. Steve used his God-given talent, his passion, and his vision to get on TV, and he is still on TV today.

Parents, I urge you to pay attention to your child grades. Find out what is happening at school. You are your child's advocate. I have had to be an advocate for my child. I was able to change his mindset, and that helped him to create a better understanding with his teacher!

Professional sports: Basketball players Michael Jordan, Kobe Bryant, Lebron James, and Tom Brady are well known. Why? What did they do differently? These athletes practiced, practiced, and practiced, always seeking to perfect their game. They learned to be team players, their aim is to win, and they are focused, disciplined, passionate, and persistent.

Jesse Owens won four gold medals in 1936, and the Jamaican sprinter Usain Bolt holds twenty-three gold medals. These athletes have one thing in common: They were passionate about winning at their game. They were willing to practice, practice, practice until they achieved their dreams. They were committed making their dreams a reality. They continue to inspire many with the legacy they leave behind!

Mechanics and engineering: Woods and Evans sold the patent for the light bulb to Thomas Edison when they didn't have the money to continue their project, which is why Thomas Edison is credited as the inventor. Willis Carrier saw the need to the lower temperature on a hot day, so he persisted and created the first air-conditioning unit. (I am so grateful!) Alexander Graham Bell saw the need for quick communication, and his vision provided the telephone—but there's more! Martin Cooper and his team created the cell phone as a way to communicate while on the go, and now we can't stop talking! All these men had a vision; they were driven and persisted until they got the results they desired!

What fuels these lives to take action to fulfill their dreams is not only passion—it's the combination of passion and persistence!

I came to the United States with my six-year-old son. I was broke, but not broken! We left all our assets behind. Sometimes, shift happens in life, and you have to make sudden changes. I was forced to make an impulsive decision because I was threatened. And when you are threatened, when you are facing the fire, you run. At that point, my material assets didn't count. It was my life and my son's life that I had to protect. I had to not only decide what was best for me, but also what would be best for my son. I had used all my God-given talent to pull myself out of a dangerous situation. I stayed on my knees, asking my God for guidance, protection, and provision! He has never failed me, and I was able to escape that situation with my son and start a new life.

I'll close this chapter with some questions for you to ask yourself. These are the same questions I asked myself. Be true to yourself and answer them today. Keep the answers as your base, and then reevaluate them at six-month intervals to see your progression.

1. What is my God given talent?
2. What is my why?
3. What is my passion?
4. How am I embracing my passion?
5. How have I invested in myself?
6. Who are my mentors ?
7. Am I hungry enough to achieve my goals to prioritize them and stay focused?
8. How have I encouraged others to embrace their dreams?

And don't forget, you need more than just passion—it's the combination of passion and persistence that will empower you to reach your own dreams!

Dr. Joan E. Wakeland is an author, international speaker, and empowerment facilitator. She is the director of the Riverside Chapter, Global Society of Female Entrepreneurs in California. She has received many awards, including the Lifetime Achievement Award from the past three presidents of the United States. Joan won the title of Ms. Elegance International in the Woman of Achievement Pageant in 2021. In 2022, Joan was awarded an honorary doctorate in humanitarianism from GIA University.

JoanEWakeland@gmail.com

Printed in the USA
CPSIA information can be obtained
at www.ICGtesting.com
LVHW051330071023
760217LV00075B/2154

9 781957 013992